Praise for *The Clean*

"'Uncle Bob' Martin definitely raises the bar with his latest book. He explains his expectation for a professional programmer on management interactions, time management, pressure, on collaboration, and on the choice of tools to use. Beyond TDD and ATDD, Martin explains what every programmer who considers him- or herself a professional not only needs to know, but also needs to follow in order to make the young profession of software development grow."

> —*Markus Gärtner*
> *Senior Software Developer*
> *it-agile GmbH*
> *www.it-agile.de*
> *www.shino.de*

"Some technical books inspire and teach; some delight and amuse. Rarely does a technical book do all four of these things. Robert Martin's always have for me and *The Clean Coder* is no exception. Read, learn, and live the lessons in this book and you can accurately call yourself a software professional."

> —*George Bullock*
> *Senior Program Manager*
> *Microsoft Corp.*

"If a computer science degree had 'required reading for after you graduate,' this would be it. In the real world, your bad code doesn't vanish when the semester's over, you don't get an A for marathon coding the night before an assignment's due, and, worst of all, you have to deal with people. So, coding gurus are not necessarily professionals. *The Clean Coder* describes the journey to professionalism . . . and it does a remarkably entertaining job of it."

> —*Jeff Overbey*
> *University of Illinois at Urbana-Champaign*

"*The Clean Coder* is much more than a set of rules or guidelines. It contains hard-earned wisdom and knowledge that is normally obtained through many years of trial and error or by working as an apprentice to a master craftsman. If you call yourself a software professional, you need this book."

> —*R. L. Bogetti*
> *Lead System Designer*
> *Baxter Healthcare*
> *www.RLBogetti.com*

The Clean Coder

The Robert C. Martin Series

PRENTICE HALL

Visit **informit.com/martinseries** for a complete list of available publications.

The Robert C. Martin Series is directed at software developers, team-leaders, business analysts, and managers who want to increase their skills and proficiency to the level of a Master Craftsman. The series contains books that guide software professionals in the principles, patterns, and practices of programming, software project management, requirements gathering, design, analysis, testing and others.

The Clean Coder

A Code of Conduct for Professional Programmers

Robert C. Martin

PRENTICE
HALL

Upper Saddle River, NJ • Boston • Indianapolis • San Francisco
New York • Toronto • Montreal • London • Munich • Paris • Madrid
Capetown • Sydney • Tokyo • Singapore • Mexico City

The publisher offers excellent discounts on this book when ordered in quantity for bulk purchases or special sales, which may include electronic versions and/or custom covers and content particular to your business, training goals, marketing focus, and branding interests. For more information, please contact:

U.S. Corporate and Government Sales
(800) 382-3419
corpsales@pearsontechgroup.com

For sales outside the United States please contact:

International Sales
international@pearson.com

Visit us on the Web: www.informit.com/ph

Library of Congress Cataloging-in-Publication Data
Martin, Robert C.
　The clean coder : a code of conduct for professional programmers / Robert Martin.
　　p.　cm.
　Includes bibliographical references and index.
　ISBN 0-13-708107-3 (pbk. : alk. paper)
1. Computer programming—Moral and ethical aspects. 2.　Computer
programmers—Professional ethics.　I. Title.
　QA76.9.M65M367 2011
　005.1092—dc22　　　　　　　　　　　　　　　　2011005962

ISBN-13: 978-0-13-708107-3
ISBN-10: 0-13-708107-3

Text printed in the United States on recycled paper at LSC Communications in Crawfordsville, Indiana.
11　18

Between 1986 and 2000 I worked closely with Jim Newkirk, a colleague from Teradyne. He and I shared a passion for programming and for clean code. We would spend nights, evenings, and weekends together playing with different programming styles and design techniques. We were continually scheming about business ideas. Eventually we formed Object Mentor, Inc., together. I learned many things from Jim as we plied our schemes together. But one of the most important was his attitude of *work ethic;* it was something I strove to emulate. Jim is a professional. I am proud to have worked with him, and to call him my friend.

CONTENTS

FOREWORD

You've picked up this book, so I assume you are a software professional. That's good; so am I. And since I have your attention, let me tell you why I picked up this book.

It all starts a short time ago in a place not too far away. Cue the curtain, lights and camera, Charley ....

Several years ago I was working at a medium-sized corporation selling highly regulated products. You know the type; we sat in a cubicle farm in a three-story building, directors and up had private offices, and getting everyone you needed into the same room for a meeting took a week or so.

We were operating in a very competitive market when the government opened up a new product.

Suddenly we had an entirely new set of potential customers; all we had to do was to get them to buy our product. That meant we had to file by a certain deadline with the federal government, pass an assessment audit by another date, and go to market on a third date.

Over and over again our management stressed to us the importance of those dates. A single slip and the government would keep us out of the market for a year, and if customers couldn't sign up on day one, then they would all sign up with someone else and we'd be out of business.

It was the sort of environment in which some people complain, and others point out that "pressure makes diamonds."

I was a technical project manager, promoted from development. My responsibility was to get the web site up on go-live day, so potential customers could download information and, most importantly, enrollment forms. My partner in the endeavor was the business-facing project manager, whom I'll call Joe. Joe's role was to work the other side, dealing with sales, marketing, and the non-technical requirements. He was also the guy fond of the "pressure makes diamonds" comment.

If you've done much work in corporate America, you've probably seen the finger-pointing, blamestorming, and work aversion that is completely natural. Our company had an interesting solution to that problem with Joe and me.

A little bit like Batman and Robin, it was our job to get things done. I met with the technical team every day in a corner; we'd rebuild the schedule every single day, figure out the critical path, then remove every possible obstacle from that critical path. If someone needed software; we'd go get it. If they would "love to" configure the firewall but "gosh, it's time for my lunch break," we would buy them lunch. If someone wanted to work on our configuration ticket but had other priorities, Joe and I would go talk to the supervisor.

Then the manager.

Then the director.

We got things done.

It's a bit of an exaggeration to say that we kicked over chairs, yelled, and screamed, but we did use every single technique in our bag to get things done, invented a few new ones along the way, and we did it in an ethical way that I am proud of to this day.

I thought of myself as a member of the team, not above jumping in to write a SQL statement or doing a little pairing to get the code out the door. At the time, I thought of Joe the same way, as a member of the team, not above it.

Eventually I came to realize that Joe did not share that opinion. That was a very sad day for me.

It was Friday at 1:00 PM; the web site was set to go live very early the following Monday.

We were done. *DONE*. Every system was go; we were ready. I had the entire tech team assembled for the final scrum meeting and we were ready to flip the switch. More than "just" the technical team, we had the business folks from marketing, the product owners, with us.

We were proud. It was a good moment.

Then Joe dropped by.

He said something like, "Bad news. Legal doesn't have the enrollment forms ready, so we can't go live yet."

This was no big deal; we'd been held up by one thing or another for the length of the entire project and had the Batman/Robin routine down pat. I was ready, and my reply was essentially, "All right partner, let's do this one more time. Legal is on the third floor, right?"

Then things got weird.

Instead of agreeing with me, Joe asked, "What are you talking about Matt?"

I said, "You know. Our usual song and dance. We're talking about four PDF files, right? That are done; legal just has to approve them? Let's go hang out in their cubicles, give them the evil eye, and get this thing *done*!"

Joe did not agree with my assessment, and answered, "We'll just go live late next week. No big deal."

You can probably guess the rest of the exchange; it sounded something like this:

> Matt: "But why? They could do this in a couple hours."
>
> Joe: "It might take more than that."
>
> Matt: "But they've got *all weekend*. Plenty of time. Let's do this!"
>
> Joe: "Matt, these are professionals. We can't just stare them down and insist they sacrifice their personal lives for our little project."
>
> Matt: (pause) "... Joe ... what do you think we've been doing to the engineering team for the past four months?"
>
> Joe: "Yes, but these are professionals."

Pause.

Breathe.

What. Did. Joe. Just. Say?

At the time, I thought the technical staff were professionals, in the best sense of the word.

Thinking back over it again, though, I'm not so sure.

Let's look at that Batman and Robin technique a second time, from a different perspective. I thought I was exhorting the team to its best performance, but I suspect Joe was playing a game, with the implicit assumption that the technical staff was his opponent. Think about it: Why was it necessary to run around, kicking over chairs and leaning on people?

Shouldn't we have been able to ask the staff when they would be done, get a firm answer, believe the answer we were given, and not be burned by that belief?

Certainly, for professionals, we should ... and, at the same time, we could not. Joe didn't trust our answers, and felt comfortable micromanaging the tech team—and at the same time, for some reason, he did trust the legal team and was not willing to micromanage them.

What's that all about?

Somehow, the legal team had demonstrated professionalism in a way the technical team had not.

Somehow, another group had convinced Joe that they did not need a babysitter, that they were not playing games, and that they needed to be treated as peers who were respected.

No, I don't think it had anything to do with fancy certificates hanging on walls or a few extra years of college, although those years of college might have included a fair bit of implicit social training on how to behave.

Ever since that day, those long years ago, I've wondered how the technical profession would have to change in order to be regarded as professionals.

Oh, I have a few ideas. I've blogged a bit, read a lot, managed to improve my own work life situation and help a few others. Yet I knew of no book that laid out a plan, that made the whole thing explicit.

Then one day, out of the blue, I got an offer to review an early draft of a book; the book that you are holding in your hands right now.

This book will tell step by step exactly how to present yourself and interact as a professional. Not with trite cliché, not with appeals to pieces of paper, but what you can do and how to do it.

In some cases, the examples are word for word.

Some of those examples have replies, counter-replies, clarifications, even advice for what to do if the other person tries to "just ignore you."

Hey, look at that, here comes Joe again, stage left this time:

Oh, here we are, back at BigCo, with Joe and me, once more on the big web site conversion project.

Only this time, imagine it just a little bit differently.

Instead of shirking from commitments, the technical staff actually makes them. Instead of shirking from estimates or letting someone else do the planning (then complaining about it), the technical team actually self-organizes and makes real commitments.

Now imagine that the staff is actually working together. When the programmers are blocked by operations, they pick up the phone and the sysadmin actually gets started on the work.

When Joe comes by to light a fire to get ticket 14321 worked on, he doesn't need to; he can see that the DBA is working diligently, not surfing the web. Likewise, the estimates he gets from staff seem downright consistent, and he doesn't get the feeling that the project is in priority somewhere between lunch and checking email. All the tricks and attempts to manipulate the schedule are not met with, "We'll try," but instead, "That's our commitment; if you want to make up your own goals, feel free."

After a while, I suspect Joe would start to think of the technical team as, well, professionals. And he'd be right.

Those steps to transform your behavior from technician to professional? You'll find them in the rest of the book.

Welcome to the next step in your career; I suspect you are going to like it.

—Matthew Heusser
Software Process Naturalist

PREFACE

At 11:39 AM EST on January 28, 1986, just 73.124 seconds after launch and at an altitude of 48,000 feet, the Space Shuttle Challenger was torn to smithereens by the failure of the right-hand solid rocket booster (SRB). Seven brave astronauts, including high school teacher Christa McAuliffe, were lost. The expression on the face of McAuliffe's mother as she watched the demise of her daughter nine miles overhead haunts me to this day.

The Challenger broke up because hot exhaust gasses in the failing SRB leaked out from between the segments of its hull, splashing across the body of the external fuel tank. The bottom of the main liquid hydrogen tank burst, igniting the fuel and driving the tank forward to smash into the liquid oxygen tank above it. At the same time the SRB detached from its aft strut and rotated around its forward strut. Its nose punctured the liquid oxygen tank. These aberrant force vectors caused the entire craft, moving well above mach 1.5, to rotate against the airstream. Aerodynamic forces quickly tore everything to shreds.

Between the circular segments of the SRB there were two concentric synthetic rubber O-rings. When the segments were bolted together the O-rings were compressed, forming a tight seal that the exhaust gasses should not have been able to penetrate.

But on the evening before the launch, the temperature on the launch pad got down to 17°F, 23 degrees below the O-rings' minimum specified temperature and 33 degrees lower than any previous launch. As a result, the O-rings grew too stiff to properly block the hot gasses. Upon ignition of the SRB there was a pressure pulse as the hot gasses rapidly accumulated. The segments of the booster ballooned outward and relaxed the compression on the O-rings. The stiffness of the O-rings prevented them from keeping the seal tight, so some of the hot gasses leaked through and vaporized the O-rings across 70 degrees of arc.

The engineers at Morton Thiokol who designed the SRB had known that there were problems with the O-rings, and they had reported those problems to managers at Morton Thiokol and NASA seven years earlier. Indeed, the O-rings from previous launches had been damaged in similar ways, though not enough to be catastrophic. The coldest launch had experienced the most damage. The engineers had designed a repair for the problem, but implementation of that repair had been long delayed.

The engineers suspected that the O-rings stiffened when cold. They also knew that temperatures for the Challenger launch were colder than any previous launch and well below the red-line. In short, the engineers *knew* that the risk was too high. The engineers acted on that knowledge. They wrote memos raising giant red flags. They strongly urged Thiokol and NASA managers not to launch. In an eleventh-hour meeting held just hours before the launch, those engineers presented their best data. They raged, and cajoled, and protested. But in the end, the managers ignored them.

When the time for launch came, some of the engineers refused to watch the broadcast because they feared an explosion on the pad. But as the Challenger climbed gracefully into the sky they began to relax. Moments before the destruction, as they watched the vehicle pass through Mach 1, one of them said that they'd "dodged a bullet."

Despite all the protest and memos, and urgings of the engineers, the managers believed they knew better. They thought the engineers were overreacting. They didn't trust the engineers' data or their conclusions. They launched because they were under immense financial and political pressure. They *hoped* everything would be just fine.

These managers were not merely foolish, they were criminal. The lives of seven good men and women, and the hopes of a generation looking toward space travel, were dashed on that cold morning because those managers set their own fears, hopes, and intuitions above the words of their own experts. They made a decision they had no right to make. They usurped the authority of the people who actually *knew*: the engineers.

But what about the engineers? Certainly the engineers did what they were supposed to do. They informed their managers and fought hard for their position. They went through the appropriate channels and invoked all the right protocols. They did what they could, *within* the system—and still the managers overrode them. So it would seem that the engineers can walk away without blame.

But sometimes I wonder whether any of those engineers lay awake at night, haunted by that image of Christa McAuliffe's mother, and wishing they'd called Dan Rather.

ABOUT THIS BOOK

This book is about software professionalism. It contains a lot of pragmatic advice in an attempt to answer questions, such as

- What is a software professional?
- How does a professional behave?
- How does a professional deal with conflict, tight schedules, and unreasonable managers?
- When, and how, should a professional say "no"?
- How does a professional deal with pressure?

But hiding within the pragmatic advice in this book you will find an attitude struggling to break through. It is an attitude of honesty, of honor, of self-respect, and of pride. It is a willingness to accept the dire responsibility of being a craftsman and an engineer. That responsibility includes working well and working clean. It includes communicating well and estimating faithfully. It includes managing your time and facing difficult risk-reward decisions.

But that responsibility includes one other thing—one frightening thing. As an engineer, you have a depth of knowledge about your systems and projects that no managers can possibly have. With that knowledge comes the responsibility to *act*.

BIBLIOGRAPHY

[**McConnell87**]: Malcolm McConnell, *Challenger 'A Major Malfunction'*, New York, NY: Simon & Schuster, 1987

[**Wiki-Challenger**]: "Space Shuttle Challenger disaster," http://en.wikipedia.org/wiki/Space_Shuttle_Challenger_disaster

ACKNOWLEDGMENTS

My career has been a series of collaborations and schemes. Though I've had many private dreams and aspirations, I always seemed to find someone to share them with. In that sense I feel a bit like the Sith, "Always two there are."

The first collaboration that I could consider professional was with John Marchese at the age of 13. He and I schemed about building computers together. I was the brains and he was the brawn. I showed him where to solder a wire and he soldered it. I showed him where to mount a relay and he mounted it. It was a load of fun, and we spent hundreds of hours at it. In fact, we built quite a few very impressive-looking objects with relays, buttons, lights, even Teletypes! Of course, none of them actually did anything, but they were very impressive and we worked very hard on them. To John: Thank you!

In my freshman year of high school I met Tim Conrad in my German class. Tim was *smart*. When we teamed up to build a computer, he was the brains and I was the brawn. He taught me electronics and gave me my first introduction to a PDP-8. He and I actually built a working electronic 18-bit binary calculator out of basic components. It could add, subtract, multiply, and divide. It took us a year of weekends and all of spring, summer, and Christmas breaks. We worked furiously on it. In the end, it worked very nicely. To Tim: Thank you!

Tim and I learned how to program computers. This wasn't easy to do in 1968, but we managed. We got books on PDP-8 assembler, Fortran, Cobol, PL/1, among others. We devoured them. We wrote programs that we had no hope of executing because we did not have access to a computer. But we wrote them anyway for the sheer love of it.

Our high school started a computer science curriculum in our sophomore year. They hooked up an ASR-33 Teletype to a 110-baud, dial-up modem. They had an account on the Univac 1108 time-sharing system at the Illinois Institute of Technology. Tim and I immediately became the de facto operators of that machine. Nobody else could get near it.

The modem was connected by picking up the telephone and dialing the number. When you heard the answering modem squeal, you pushed the "orig" button on the Teletype causing the originating modem to emit its own squeal. Then you hung up the phone and the data connection was established.

The phone had a lock on the dial. Only the teachers had the key. But that didn't matter, because we learned that you could dial a phone (any phone) by tapping out the phone number on the switch hook. I was a drummer, so I had pretty good timing and reflexes. I could dial that modem, with the lock in place, in less than 10 seconds.

We had two Teletypes in the computer lab. One was the online machine and the other was an offline machine. Both were used by students to write their programs. The students would type their programs on the Teletypes with the paper tape punch engaged. Every keystroke was punched on tape. The students wrote their programs in IITran, a remarkably powerful interpreted language. Students would leave their paper tapes in a basket near the Teletypes.

After school, Tim and I would dial up the computer (by tapping of course), load the tapes into the IITran batch system, and then hang up. At 10 characters per second, this was not a quick procedure. An hour or so later, we'd call back and get the printouts, again at 10 characters per second. The Teletype did not separate the students' listings by ejecting pages. It just printed one after the next after the next, so we cut them apart using scissors, paper-clipped their input paper tape to their listing, and put them in the output basket.

Tim and I were the masters and gods of that process. Even the teachers left us alone when we were in that room. We were doing their job, and they knew it. They never asked us to do it. They never told us we could. They never gave us the key to the phone. We just moved in, and they moved out—and they gave us a very long leash. To my Math teachers, Mr. McDermit, Mr. Fogel, and Mr. Robien: Thank you!

Then, after all the student homework was done, we would play. We wrote program after program to do any number of mad and weird things. We wrote programs that graphed circles and parabolas in ASCII on a Teletype. We wrote random walk programs and random word generators. We calculated 50 factorial to the last digit. We spent hours and hours inventing programs to write and then getting them to work.

Two years later, Tim, our compadre Richard Lloyd, and I were hired as programmers at ASC Tabulating in Lake Bluff, Illinois. Tim and I were 18 at the time. We had decided that college was a waste of time and that we should begin our careers immediately. It was here that we met Bill Hohri, Frank Ryder, Big Jim Carlin, and John Miller. They gave some youngsters the opportunity to learn what professional programming was all about. The experience was not all positive and not all negative. It was certainly educational. To all of them, and to Richard who catalyzed and drove much of that process: Thank you.

After quitting and melting down at the age of 20, I did a stint as a lawn mower repairman working for my brother-in-law. I was so bad at it that he had to fire me. Thanks, Wes!

A year or so later I wound up working at Outboard Marine Corporation. By this time I was married and had a baby on the way. They fired me too. Thanks, John, Ralph, and Tom!

Then I went to work at Teradyne where I met Russ Ashdown, Ken Finder, Bob Copithorne, Chuck Studee, and CK Srithran (now Kris Iyer). Ken was my boss. Chuck and CK were my buds. I learned so much from all of them. Thanks, guys!

Then there was Mike Carew. At Teradyne, he and I became the dynamic duo. We wrote several systems together. If you wanted to get something done, and done fast, you got Bob and Mike to do it. We had a load of fun together. Thanks, Mike!

Jerry Fitzpatrick also worked at Teradyne. We met while playing Dungeons & Dragons together, but quickly formed a collaboration. We wrote software on a Commodore 64 to support D&D users. We also started a new project at Teradyne called "The Electronic Receptionist." We worked together for several years, and he became, and remains, a great friend. Thanks, Jerry!

I spent a year in England while working for Teradyne. There I teamed up with Mike Kergozou. He and I schemed together about all manner of things, though most of those schemes had to do with bicycles and pubs. But he was a dedicated programmer who was very focused on quality and discipline (though, perhaps he would disagree). Thanks, Mike!

Returning from England in 1987, I started scheming with Jim Newkirk. We both left Teradyne (months apart) and joined a start-up named Clear Communications. We spent several years together there toiling to make the millions that never came. But we continued our scheming. Thanks, Jim!

In the end we founded Object Mentor together. Jim is the most direct, disciplined, and focused person with whom I've ever had the privilege to work. He taught me so many things, I can't enumerate them here. Instead, I have dedicated this book to him.

There are so many others I've schemed with, so many others I've collaborated with, so many others who have had an impact on my professional life: Lowell Lindstrom, Dave Thomas, Michael Feathers, Bob Koss, Brett Schuchert, Dean Wampler, Pascal Roy, Jeff Langr, James Grenning, Brian Button, Alan Francis,

Mike Hill, Eric Meade, Ron Jeffries, Kent Beck, Martin Fowler, Grady Booch, and an endless list of others. Thank you, one and all.

Of course, the greatest collaborator of my life has been my lovely wife, Ann Marie. I married her when I was 20, three days after she turned 18. For 38 years she has been my steady companion, my rudder and sail, my love and my life. I look forward to another four decades with her.

And now, my collaborators and scheming partners are my children. I work closely with my eldest daughter Angela, my lovely mother hen and intrepid assistant. She keeps me on the straight and narrow and never lets me forget a date or commitment. I scheme business plans with my son Micah, the founder of 8thlight.com. His head for business is far better than mine ever was. Our latest venture, cleancoders.com, is very exciting!

My younger son Justin has just started working with Micah at 8th Light. My younger daughter Gina is a chemical engineer working for Honeywell. With those two, the serious scheming has just begun!

No one in your life will teach you more than your children will. Thanks, kids!

ABOUT THE AUTHOR

Robert C. Martin (**"Uncle Bob"**) has been a programmer since 1970. He is founder and president of Object Mentor, Inc., an international firm of highly experienced software developers and managers who specialize in helping companies get their projects done. Object Mentor offers process improvement consulting, object-oriented software design consulting, training, and skill development services to major corporations worldwide.

Martin has published dozens of articles in various trade journals and is a regular speaker at international conferences and trade shows.

He has authored and edited many books, including:

- *Designing Object Oriented C++ Applications Using the Booch Method*
- *Patterns Languages of Program Design 3*

- *More C++ Gems*
- *Extreme Programming in Practice*
- *Agile Software Development: Principles, Patterns, and Practices*
- *UML for Java Programmers*
- *Clean Code*

A leader in the industry of software development, Martin served for three years as editor-in-chief of the *C++ Report*, and he served as the first chairman of the Agile Alliance.

Robert is also the founder of Uncle Bob Consulting, LLC, and cofounder with his son Micah Martin of The Clean Coders LLC.

ON THE COVER

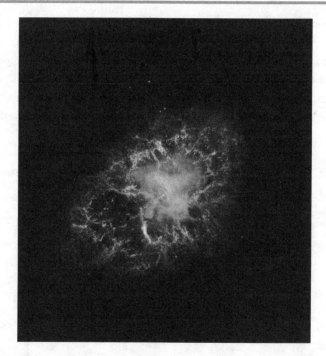

The stunning image on the cover, reminiscent of Sauron's eye, is M1, the Crab Nebula. M1 is located in Taurus, about one degree to the right of Zeta Tauri, the star at the tip of the bull's left horn. The crab nebula is the remnant of a supernova that blew its guts all over the sky on the rather auspicious date of July 4th, 1054 AD. At a distance of 6500 light years, that explosion appeared to Chinese observers as a new star, roughly as bright as Jupiter. Indeed, it was visible *during the day*! Over the next six months it slowly faded from naked-eye view.

The cover image is a composite of visible and x-ray light. The visible image was taken by the Hubble telescope and forms the outer envelope. The inner object that looks like a blue archery target was taken by the Chandra x-ray telescope.

The visible image depicts a rapidly expanding cloud of dust and gas laced with heavy elements left over from the supernova explosion. That cloud is now 11 light-years in diameter, weighs in at 4.5 solar masses, and is expanding at the furious rate of 1500 kilometers per second. The kinetic energy of that old explosion is impressive to say the least.

At the very center of the target is a bright blue dot. That's where the *pulsar* is. It was the formation of the pulsar that caused the star to blow up in the first place. Nearly a solar mass of material in the core of the doomed star imploded into a sphere of neutrons about 30 kilometers in diameter. The kinetic energy of that implosion, coupled with the incredible barrage of neutrinos created when all those neutrons formed, ripped the star open, and blew it to kingdom come.

The pulsar is spinning about 30 times per second; and it flashes as it spins. We can see it blinking in our telescopes. Those pulses of light are the reason we call it a pulsar, which is short for Pulsating Star.

PRE-REQUISITE INTRODUCTION

(Don't skip this, you're going to need it.)

I presume you just picked up this book because you are a computer programmer and are intrigued by the notion of professionalism. You should be. Professionalism is something that our profession is in dire need of.

I'm a programmer too. I've been a programmer for 42[1] years; and in that time—*let me tell you*—I've seen it all. I've been fired. I've been lauded. I've been a team leader, a manager, a grunt, and even a CEO. I've worked with brilliant

---

1. Don't Panic.

programmers and I've worked with slugs.[2] I've worked on high-tech cutting-edge embedded software/hardware systems, and I've worked on corporate payroll systems. I've programmed in COBOL, FORTRAN, BAL, PDP-8, PDP-11, C, C++, Java, Ruby, Smalltalk, and a plethora of other languages and systems. I've worked with untrustworthy paycheck thieves, and I've worked with consummate professionals. It is that last classification that is the topic of this book.

In the pages of this book I will try to define what it means to be a professional programmer. I will describe the attitudes, disciplines, and actions that I consider to be essentially professional.

How do I know what these attitudes, disciplines, and actions are? Because I had to learn them the hard way. You see, when I got my first job as a programmer, professional was the last word you'd have used to describe me.

The year was 1969. I was 17. My father had badgered a local business named ASC into hiring me as a temporary part-time programmer. (Yes, my father could do things like that. I once watched him walk out in front of a speeding car with his hand out commanding it to "Stop!" The car stopped. Nobody said "no" to my Dad.) The company put me to work in the room where all the IBM computer manuals were kept. They had me put years and years of updates into the manuals. It was here that I first saw the phrase: "This page intentionally left blank."

After a couple of days of updating manuals, my supervisor asked me to write a simple Easycoder[3] program. I was thrilled to be asked. I'd never written a program for a real computer before. I had, however, inhaled the Autocoder books, and had a vague notion of how to begin.

The program was simply to read records from a tape, and replace the IDs of those records with new IDs. The new IDs started at 1 and were incremented by

---

2. A technical term of unknown origins.
3. Easycoder was the assembler for the Honeywell H200 computer, which was similar to Autocoder for the IBM 1401 computer.

1 for each new record. The records with the new IDs were to be written to a new tape.

My supervisor showed me a shelf that held many stacks of red and blue punched cards. Imagine that you bought 50 decks of playing cards, 25 red decks, and 25 blue decks. Then you stacked those decks one on top of the other. That's what these stacks of cards looked like. They were striped red and blue, and the stripes were about 200 cards each. Each one of those stripes contained the source code for the subroutine library that the programmers typically used. Programmers would simply take the top deck off the stack, making sure that they took nothing but red or blue cards, and then put that at the end of their program deck.

I wrote my program on some coding forms. Coding forms were large rectangular sheets of paper divided into 25 lines and 80 columns. Each line represented one card. You wrote your program on the coding form using block capital letters and a #2 pencil. In the last 6 columns of each line you wrote a sequence number with that #2 pencil. Typically you incremented the sequence number by 10 so that you could insert cards later.

The coding form went to the key punchers. This company had several dozen women who took coding forms from a big in-basket, and then "typed" them into key-punch machines. These machines were a lot like typewriters, except that the characters were punched into cards instead of printed on paper.

The next day the keypunchers returned my program to me by inter-office mail. My small deck of punched cards was wrapped up by my coding forms and a rubber band. I looked over the cards for keypunch errors. There weren't any. So then I put the subroutine library deck on the end of my program deck, and then took the deck upstairs to the computer operators.

The computers were behind locked doors in an environmentally controlled room with a raised floor (for all the cables). I knocked on the door and an operator austerely took my deck from me and put it into another in-basket inside the computer room. When they got around to it, they would run my deck.

The next day I got my deck back. It was wrapped in a listing of the results of the run and kept together with a rubber band. (We used *lots* of rubber bands in those days!)

I opened the listing and saw that my compile had failed. The error messages in the listing were very difficult for me to understand, so I took it to my supervisor. He looked it over, mumbled under his breath, made some quick notes on the listing, grabbed my deck and then told me to follow him.

He took me up to the keypunch room and sat at a vacant keypunch machine. One by one he corrected the cards that were in error, and added one or two other cards. He quickly explained what he was doing, but it all went by like a flash.

He took the new deck up to the computer room and knocked at the door. He said some magic words to one of the operators, and then walked into the computer room behind him. He beckoned for me to follow. The operator set up the tape drives and loaded the deck while we watched. The tapes spun, the printer chattered, and then it was over. The program had worked.

The next day my supervisor thanked me for my help, and terminated my employment. Apparently ASC didn't feel they had the time to nurture a 17-year-old.

But my connection with ASC was hardly over. A few months later I got a full-time second-shift job at ASC operating off-line printers. These printers printed junk mail from print images that were stored on tape. My job was to load the printers with paper, load the tapes into the tape drives, fix paper jams, and otherwise just watch the machines work.

The year was 1970. College was not an option for me, nor did it hold any particular enticements. The Viet Nam war was still raging, and the campuses were chaotic. I had continued to inhale books on COBOL, Fortran, PL/1, PDP-8, and IBM 360 Assembler. My intent was to bypass school and drive as hard as I could to get a job programming.

Twelve months later I achieved that goal. I was promoted to a full-time programmer at ASC. I, and two of my good friends, Richard and Tim, also 19, worked with a team of three other programmers writing a real-time accounting system for a teamster's union. The machine was a Varian 620i. It was a simple mini-computer similar in architecture to a PDP-8 except that it had a 16-bit word and two registers. The language was assembler.

We wrote every line of code in that system. And I mean *every* line. We wrote the operating system, the interrupt heads, the IO drivers, the *file system* for the disks, the overlay swapper, and even the relocatable linker. Not to mention all the application code. We wrote all this in 8 months working 70 and 80 hours a week to meet a hellish deadline. My salary was $7,200 per year.

We delivered that system. And then we quit.

We quit suddenly, and with malice. You see, after all that work, and after having delivered a successful system, the company gave us a 2% raise. We felt cheated and abused. Several of us got jobs elsewhere and simply resigned.

I, however, took a different, and very unfortunate, approach. I and a buddy stormed into the boss' office and quit together rather loudly. This was emotionally very satisfying—for a day.

The next day it hit me that I did not have a job. I was 19, unemployed, with no degree. I interviewed for a few programming positions, but those interviews did not go well. So I worked in my brother-in-law's lawnmower repair shop for four months. Unfortunately I was a lousy lawnmower repairman. He eventually had to let me go. I fell into a nasty funk.

I stayed up till 3 AM every night eating pizza and watching old monster movies on my parents' old black-and-white, rabbit-ear TV. Only some of the ghosts where characters in the movies. I stayed in bed till 1 PM because I didn't want to face my dreary days. I took a calculus course at a local community college and failed it. I was a wreck.

My mother took me aside and told me that my life was a mess, and that I had been an idiot for quitting without having a new job, and for quitting so emotionally, and for quitting together with my buddy. She told me that you never quit without having a new job, and you always quit calmly, coolly, and alone. She told me that I should call my old boss and beg for my old job back. She said, "You need to eat some humble pie."

Nineteen-year-old boys are not known for their appetite for humble pie, and I was no exception. But the circumstances had taken their toll on my pride. In the end I called my boss and took a big bite of that humble pie. And it worked. He was happy to re-hire me for $6,800 per year, and I was happy to take it.

I spent another eighteen months working there, watching my Ps and Qs and trying to be as valuable an employee as I could. I was rewarded with promotions and raises, and a regular paycheck. Life was good. When I left that company, it was on good terms, and with an offer for a better job in my pocket.

You might think that I had learned my lesson; that I was now a professional. Far from it. That was just the first of many lessons I needed to learn. In the coming years I would be fired from one job for carelessly missing critical dates, and nearly fired from still another for inadvertently leaking confidential information to a customer. I would take the lead on a doomed project and ride it into the ground without calling for the help I knew I needed. I would aggressively defend my technical decisions even though they flew in the face of the customers' needs. I would hire one wholly unqualified person, saddling my employer with a huge liability to deal with. And worst of all, I would get two other people fired because of my inability to lead.

So think of this book as a catalog of my own errors, a blotter of my own crimes, and a set of guidelines for you to avoid walking in my early shoes.

1 PROFESSIONALISM

"Oh laugh, Curtin, old boy. It's a great joke played on us by the Lord, or fate, or nature, whatever you prefer. But whoever or whatever played it certainly had a sense of humor! Ha!"

— *Howard,* The Treasure of the Sierra Madre

So, you want to be a professional software developer do you? You want to hold your head high and declare to the world: "I am a *professional!*" You want people to look at you with respect and treat you with deference. You want mothers pointing at you and telling their children to be like you. You want it all. Right?

BE CAREFUL WHAT YOU ASK FOR

Professionalism is a loaded term. Certainly it is a badge of honor and pride, but it is also a marker of responsibility and accountability. The two go hand in hand, of course. You can't take pride and honor in something that you can't be held accountable for.

It's a lot easier to be a nonprofessional. Nonprofessionals don't have to take responsibility for the job they do—they leave that to their employers. If a nonprofessional makes an error, the employer cleans up the mess. But when a professional makes a mistake, *he* cleans up the mess.

What would happen if you allowed a bug to slip through a module, and it cost your company $10,000? The nonprofessional would shrug his shoulders, say "stuff happens," and start writing the next module. The professional would write the company a check for $10,000![1]

Yeah, it feels a little different when it's your own money, doesn't it? But that feeling is the feeling a professional has all the time. Indeed, that feeling is the essence of professionalism. Because, you see, professionalism is all about taking responsibility.

TAKING RESPONSIBILITY

You read the introduction, right? If not, go back and do so now; it sets the context for everything that follows in this book.

I learned about taking responsibility by suffering through the consequences of not taking it.

---

1. Hopefully he has a good Errors and Omissions policy!

In 1979 I was working for a company named Teradyne. I was the "responsible engineer" for the software that controlled a mini- and microcomputer-based system that measured the quality of telephone lines. The central mini-computer was connected via 300-baud dedicated or dial-up phone lines to dozens of satellite micro-computers that controlled the measurement hardware. The code was all written in assembler.

Our customers were the service managers of major telephone companies. Each had the responsibility for 100,000 telephone lines or more. My system helped these service area managers find and repair malfunctions and problems in the telephone lines before their customers noticed them. This reduced the customer complaint rates that the public utility commissions measured and used to regulate the rates that the telephone companies could charge. In short, these systems were incredibly important.

Every night these systems ran through a "nightly routine" in which the central mini-computer told each of the satellite micro-computers to test every telephone line under their control. Each morning the central computer would pull back the list of faulty lines, along with their failing characteristics. The service area managers would use this report to schedule repairmen to fix the faults before the customers could complain.

On one occasion I shipped a new release to several dozen customers. "Ship" is exactly the right word. I wrote the software onto tapes and shipped those tapes to the customers. The customers loaded the tapes and then rebooted the systems.

The new release fixed some minor defects and added a new feature that our customers had been demanding. We had told them we would provide that new feature by a certain date. I barely managed to overnight the tapes so that they'd arrive on the promised date.

Two days later I got a call from our field service manager, Tom. He told me that several customers had complained that the "nightly routine" had not completed, and that they had gotten no reports. My heart sank because in order to ship the software on time, I had neglected to test the routine. I had tested much of the other functionality of the system, but testing the routine took hours, and I needed to ship the software. None of the bug fixes were in the routine code, so I felt safe.

Losing a nightly report was a *big deal.* It meant that the repairmen had less to do and would be overbooked later. It meant that some customers might notice a fault and complain. Losing a night's worth of data is enough to get a service area manager to call Tom and lambaste him.

I fired up our lab system, loaded the new software, and then started a routine. It took several hours but then it aborted. The routine failed. Had I run this test before I shipped, the service areas wouldn't have lost data, and the service area managers wouldn't be roasting Tom right now.

I phoned Tom to tell him that I could duplicate the problem. He told me that most of the other customers had called him with the same complaint. Then he asked me when I could fix it. I told him I didn't know, but that I was working on it. In the meantime I told him that the customers should go back to the old software. He was angry at me saying that this was a double blow to the customers since they'd lost a whole night's worth of data and couldn't use the new feature they were promised.

The bug was hard to find, and testing took several hours. The first fix didn't work. Nor did the second. It took me several tries, and therefore several days, to figure out what had gone wrong. The whole time, Tom was calling me every few hours asking me when I'd have this fixed. He also made sure I knew about the earfuls he was getting from the service area managers, and just how embarrassing it was for him to tell them to put the old tapes back in.

In the end, I found the defect, shipped the new tapes, and everything went back to normal. Tom, who was not my boss, cooled down and we put the whole episode behind us. My boss came to me when it was over and said, "I bet you aren't going to do that again." I agreed.

Upon reflection I realized that shipping without testing the routine had been irresponsible. The reason I neglected the test was so I could say I had shipped on time. It was about me saving face. I had not been concerned about the customer, nor about my employer. I had only been concerned about my own reputation. I should have taken responsibility early and told Tom that the tests weren't complete and that I was not prepared to ship the software on time. That would have been hard, and Tom would have been upset. But no customers would have lost data, and no service managers would have called.

FIRST, DO NO HARM

So how do we take responsibility? There are some principles. Drawing from the Hippocratic oath may seem arrogant, but what better source is there? And, indeed, doesn't it make sense that the first responsibility, and first goal, of an aspiring professional is to use his or her powers for good?

What harm can a software developer do? From a purely software point of view, he or she can do harm to both the function and structure of the software. We'll explore how to avoid doing just that.

DO NO HARM TO FUNCTION

Clearly, we want our software to work. Indeed, most of us are programmers today because we got something to work once and we want that feeling again. But we aren't the only ones who want the software to work. Our customers and employers want it to work too. Indeed, they are paying us to create software that works just the way they want it to.

We harm the function of our software when we create bugs. Therefore, in order to be professional, we must not create bugs.

"But wait!" I hear you say. "That's not reasonable. Software is too complex to create without bugs."

Of course you are right. Software *is* too complex to create without bugs. Unfortunately that doesn't let you off the hook. The human body is too complex to understand in it's entirety, but doctors still take an oath to do no harm. If they don't take themselves off a hook like *that*, how can we?

"Are you telling us we must be perfect?" Do I hear you object?

No, I'm telling you that you must be responsible for your imperfections. The fact that bugs will certainly occur in your code does not mean you aren't responsible for them. The fact that the task to write perfect software is virtually impossible does not mean you aren't responsible for the imperfection.

It is the lot of a professional to be accountable for errors even though errors are virtually certain. So, my aspiring professional, the first thing you must practice is apologizing. Apologies are necessary, but insufficient. You cannot simply keep making the same errors over and over. As you mature in your profession, your error rate should rapidly decrease towards the asymptote of zero. It won't ever get to zero, but it is your responsibility to get as close as possible to it.

QA Should Find Nothing

Therefore, when you release your software you should expect QA to find no problems. It is unprofessional in the extreme to purposely send code that you know to be faulty to QA. And what code do you know to be faulty? Any code you aren't *certain* about!

Some folks use QA as the bug catchers. They send them code that they haven't thoroughly checked. They depend on QA to find the bugs and report them back to the developers. Indeed, some companies reward QA based on the number of bugs they find. The more bugs, the greater the reward.

Never mind that this is a desperately expensive behavior that damages the company and the software. Never mind that this behavior ruins schedules and undermines the confidence of the enterprise in the development team. Never mind that this behavior is just plain lazy and irresponsible. Releasing code to QA that you don't know works is unprofessional. It violates the "do no harm" rule.

Will QA find bugs? Probably, so get ready to apologize—and then figure out why those bugs managed to escape your notice and do something to prevent it from happening again.

Every time QA, or worse a *user*, finds a problem, you should be surprised, chagrined, and determined to prevent it from happening again.

You Must *Know* It Works

How can you *know* your code works? That's easy. Test it. Test it again. Test it up. Test it down. Test it seven ways to Sunday!

Perhaps you are concerned that testing your code so much will take too much time. After all you've got schedules and deadlines to keep. If you spend all your time testing, you'll never get anything else written. Good point! So, automate your tests. Write unit tests that you can execute on a moment's notice, and run those tests as often as you can.

How much of the code should be tested with these automated unit tests? Do I really need to answer that question? All of it! All. Of. It.

Am I suggesting 100% test coverage? No, I'm not *suggesting* it. I'm *demanding* it. Every single line of code that you write should be tested. Period.

Isn't that unrealistic? Of course not. You only write code because you expect it to get executed. If you expect it to get executed, you ought to *know* that it works. The only way to know this is to test it.

I am the primary contributor and committer for an open source project called FITNESSE. As of this writing there are 60ksloc in FITNESSE. 26 of those 60 are written in 2000+ unit tests. Emma reports that the coverage of those 2000 tests is ~90%.

Why isn't my code coverage higher? Because Emma can't see all the lines of code that are being executed! I believe the coverage is much higher than that. Is the coverage 100%? No, 100% is an asymptote.

But isn't some code hard to test? Yes, but only because that code has been *designed* to be hard to test. The solution to that is to design your code to be *easy* to test. And the best way to do that is to write your tests first, before you write the code that passes them.

This is a discipline known as Test Driven Development (TDD), which we will say more about in a later chapter.

Automated QA

The entire QA procedure for FITNESSE is the execution of the unit and acceptance tests. If those tests pass, I ship. This means my QA procedure takes about three minutes, and I can execute it on a whim.

Now, it's true that nobody dies if there is a bug in FITNESSE. Nobody loses millions of dollars either. On the other hand, FITNESSE has many thousands of users, and a *very* small bug list.

Certainly some systems are so mission-critical that a short automated test is insufficient to determine readiness for deployment. On the other hand, you as a developer need a relatively quick and reliable mechanism to know that the code you have written works and does not interfere with the rest of the system. So, at the very least, your automated tests should tell you that the system is *very likely* to pass QA.

DO NO HARM TO STRUCTURE

The true professional knows that delivering function at the expense of structure is a fool's errand. It is the structure of your code that allows it to be flexible. If you compromise the structure, you compromise the future.

The fundamental assumption underlying all software projects is that software is easy to change. If you violate this assumption by creating inflexible structures, then you undercut the economic model that the entire industry is based on.

In short: *You must be able to make changes without exorbitant costs.*

Unfortunately, all too many projects become mired in a tar pit of poor structure. Tasks that used to take days begin to take weeks, and then months. Management, desperate to recapture lost momentum, hires more developers to speed things up. But these developers simply add to the morass, deepening the structural damage and raising the impediment.

Much has been written about the principles and patterns of software design that support structures that are flexible and maintainable.[2] Professional software developers commit these things to memory and strive to conform their software to them. But there's a trick to this that far too few software developers follow: *If you want your software to be flexible, you have to flex it!*

The only way to prove that your software is easy to change is to make easy changes to it. And when you find that the changes aren't as easy as you thought, you refine the design so that the next change is easier.

When do you make these easy changes? *All the time!* Every time you look at a module you make small, lightweight changes to it to improve its structure. Every time you read through the code you adjust the structure.

This philosophy is sometimes called *merciless refactoring*. I call it "the Boy Scout rule": Always check in a module cleaner than when you checked it out. Always make some random act of kindness to the code whenever you see it.

This is completely counter to the way most people think about software. They think that making a continuous series of changes to working software is *dangerous*. No! What is dangerous is allowing the software to remain static. If you aren't flexing it, then when you *do* need to change it, you'll find it rigid.

Why do most developers fear to make continuous changes to their code? They are afraid they'll break it! Why are they afraid they'll break it? Because they don't have tests.

It all comes back to the tests. If you have an automated suite of tests that covers virtually 100% of the code, and if that suite of tests can be executed quickly on a whim, then *you simply will not be afraid to change the code.* How do you prove you are not afraid to change the code? You change it all the time.

Professional developers are so certain of their code and tests that they are maddeningly casual about making random, opportunistic changes. They'll change the name of a class, on a whim. They'll notice a long-ish method while

---

2. [PPP2001]

reading through a module and repartition it as a matter of course. They'll transform a switch statement into polymorphic deployment, or collapse an inheritance hierarchy into a chain-of-command. In short, they treat software the way a sculptor treats clay—they continuously shape and mold it.

WORK ETHIC

Your career is *your* responsibility. It is not your employer's responsibility to make sure you are marketable. It is not your employer's responsibility to train you, or to send you to conferences, or to buy you books. These things are *your* responsibility. Woe to the software developer who entrusts his career to his employer.

Some employers are willing to buy you books and send you to training classes and conferences. That's fine, they are doing you a favor. But never fall into the trap of thinking that this is your employer's responsibility. If your employer doesn't do these things for you, you should find a way to do them yourself.

It is also not your employer's responsibility to give you the time you need to learn. Some employers may provide that time. Some employers may even demand that you take the time. But again, they are doing you a favor, and you should be appropriately appreciative. Such favors are not something you should expect.

You owe your employer a certain amount of time and effort. For the sake of argument, let's use the U.S. standard of 40 hours per week. These 40 hours should be spent on *your employer's* problems, not on *your* problems.

You should plan on working 60 hours per week. The first 40 are for your employer. The remaining 20 are for you. During this remaining 20 hours you should be reading, practicing, learning, and otherwise enhancing your career.

I can hear you thinking: "But what about my family? What about my life? Am I supposed to sacrifice them for my employer?"

I'm not talking about *all* your free time here. I'm talking about 20 extra hours per week. That's roughly three hours per day. If you use your lunch hour to read, listen to podcasts on your commute, and spend 90 minutes per day learning a new language, you'll have it all covered.

Do the math. In a week there are 168 hours. Give your employer 40, and your career another 20. That leaves 108. Another 56 for sleep leaves 52 for everything else.

Perhaps you don't want to make that kind of commitment. That's fine, but you should not then think of yourself as a professional. Professionals spend *time* caring for their profession.

Perhaps you think that work should stay at work and that you shouldn't bring it home. I agree! You should not be working for your employer during those 20 hours. Instead, you should be working on your career.

Sometimes these two are aligned with each other. Sometimes the work you do for your employer is greatly beneficial to your career. In that case, spending some of that 20 hours on it is reasonable. But remember, those 20 hours are for *you*. They are to be used to make yourself more valuable as a professional.

Perhaps you think this is a recipe for burnout. On the contrary, it is a recipe to *avoid* burnout. Presumably you became a software developer because you are passionate about software and your desire to be a professional is motivated by that passion. During that 20 hours you should be doing those things that *reinforce* that passion. Those 20 hours should be *fun!*

KNOW YOUR FIELD

Do you know what a Nassi-Shneiderman chart is? If not, why not? Do you know the difference between a Mealy and a Moore state machine? You should. Could you write a quicksort without looking it up? Do you know what the term "Transform Analysis" means? Could you perform a functional decomposition with Data Flow Diagrams? What does the term "Tramp Data" mean? Have you heard the term "Conascence"? What is a Parnas Table?

A wealth of ideas, disciplines, techniques, tools, and terminologies decorate the last fifty years of our field. How much of this do you know? If you want to be a professional, you should know a sizable chunk of it and constantly be increasing the size of that chunk.

Why should you know these things? After all, isn't our field progressing so rapidly that all these old ideas have become irrelevant? The first part of that query seems obvious on the surface. Certainly our field is progressing and at a ferocious pace. Interestingly enough, however, that progress is in many respects peripheral. It's true that we don't wait 24 hours for compile turnaround any more. It's true that we write systems that are gigabytes in size. It's true that we work in the midst of a globe-spanning network that provides instant access to information. On the other hand, we are writing the same `if` and `while` statements that we were writing 50 years ago. Much has changed. Much has not.

The second part of the query is certainly not true. Very few ideas of the past 50 years have become irrelevant. Some have been sidelined, it's true. The notion of doing waterfall development has certainly fallen into disfavor. But that doesn't mean we shouldn't know what it is, and what its good and bad points are.

Overall, however, the vast majority of the hard-won ideas of the last 50 years are as valuable today as they were then. Perhaps they are even more valuable now.

Remember Santayana's curse: "Those who cannot remember the past are condemned to repeat it."

Here is a *minimal* list of the things that every software professional should be conversant with:

- Design patterns. You ought to be able to describe all 24 patterns in the GOF book and have a working knowledge of many of the patterns in the POSA books.
- Design principles. You should know the SOLID principles and have a good understanding of the component principles.
- Methods. You should understand XP, Scrum, Lean, Kanban, Waterfall, Structured Analysis, and Structured Design.

- Disciplines. You should practice TDD, Object-Oriented design, Structured Programming, Continuous Integration, and Pair Programming.
- Artifacts: You should know how to use: UML, DFDs, Structure Charts, Petri Nets, State Transition Diagrams and Tables, flow charts, and decision tables.

CONTINUOUS LEARNING

The frenetic rate of change in our industry means that software developers must continue to learn copious quantities just to keep up. Woe to the architects who stop coding—they will rapidly find themselves irrelevant. Woe to the programmers who stop learning new languages—they will watch as the industry passes them by. Woe to the developers who fail to learn new disciplines and techniques—their peers will excel as they decline.

Would you visit a doctor who did not keep current with medical journals? Would you hire a tax lawyer who did not keep current with the tax laws and precedents? Why should employers hire developers who don't keep current?

Read books, articles, blogs, tweets. Go to conferences. Go to user groups. Participate in reading and study groups. Learn things that are outside your comfort zone. If you are a .NET programmer, learn Java. If you are a Java programmer, learn Ruby. If you are a C programmer, learn Lisp. If you want to really bend your brain, learn Prolog and Forth!

PRACTICE

Professionals practice. True professionals work hard to keep their skills sharp and ready. It is not enough to simply do your daily job and call that practice. Doing your daily job is performance, not practice. Practice is when you specifically exercise your skills *outside* of the performance of your job for the sole purpose of refining and enhancing those skills.

What could it possibly mean for a software developer to practice? At first thought the concept seems absurd. But stop and think for a moment. Consider how musicians master their craft. It's not by performing. It's by practicing. And how do they practice? Among other things, they have special exercises that they perform. Scales and etudes and runs. They do these over and over to train their fingers and their mind, and to maintain mastery of their skill.

So what could software developers do to practice? There's a whole chapter in this book dedicated to different practice techniques, so I won't go into much detail here. One technique I use frequently is the repetition of simple exercises such as the `Bowling Game` or `Prime Factors`. I call these exercises *kata*. There are many such kata to choose from.

A kata usually comes in the form of a simple programming problem to solve, such as writing the function that calculates the prime factors of an integer. The point of doing the kata is not to figure out how to solve the problem; you know how to do that already. The point of the kata is to train your fingers and your brain.

I'll do a kata or two every day, often as part of settling in to work. I might do it in Java, or in Ruby, or in Clojure, or in some other language for which I want to maintain my skills. I'll use the kata to sharpen a particular skill, such as keeping my fingers used to hitting shortcut keys, or using certain refactorings.

Think of the kata as a 10-minute warm-up exercise in the morning and a 10-minute cool-down in the evening.

COLLABORATION

The second best way to learn is to collaborate with other people. Professional software developers make a special effort to program together, practice together, design and plan together. By doing so they learn a lot from each other, and they get more done faster with fewer errors.

This doesn't mean you have to spend 100% of your time working with others. Alone time is also very important. As much as I like to pair program with others, it makes me crazy if I can't get away by myself from time to time.

MENTORING

The best way to learn is to teach. Nothing will drive facts and values into your head faster and harder than having to communicate them to people you are responsible for. So the benefit of teaching is strongly in favor of the teacher.

By the same token, there is no better way to bring new people into an organization than to sit down with them and show them the ropes. Professionals take personal responsibility for mentoring juniors. They will not let a junior flail about unsupervised.

Know Your Domain

It is the responsibility of every software professional to understand the domain of the solutions they are programming. If you are writing an accounting system, you should know the accounting field. If you are writing a travel application, you should know the travel industry. You don't have to be a domain expert, but there is a reasonable amount of due diligence that you ought to engage in.

When starting a project in a new domain, read a book or two on the topic. Interview your customer and users about the foundation and basics of the domain. Spend some time with the experts, and try to understand their principles and values.

It is the worst kind of unprofessional behavior to simply code from a spec without understanding why that spec makes sense to the business. Rather, you should know enough about the domain to be able to recognize and challenge specification errors.

Identify with Your Employer/Customer

Your employer's problems are *your* problems. You need to understand what those problems are and work toward the best solutions. As you develop a system you need to put yourself in your employer's shoes and make sure that the features you are developing are really going to address your employer's needs.

It is easy for developers to identify with each other. It's easy to fall into an *us versus them* attitude with your employer. Professionals avoid this at all costs.

HUMILITY

Programming is an act of creation. When we write code we are creating something out of nothing. We are boldly imposing order upon chaos. We are confidently commanding, in precise detail, the behaviors of a machine that could otherwise do incalculable damage. And so, programming is an act of supreme arrogance.

Professionals know they are arrogant and are not falsely humble. A professional knows his job and takes pride in his work. A professional is confident in his abilities, and takes bold and calculated risks based on that confidence. A professional is not timid.

However, a professional also knows that there will be times when he will fail, his risk calculations will be wrong, his abilities will fall short; he'll look in the mirror and see an arrogant fool smiling back at him.

So when a professional finds himself the butt of a joke, he'll be the first to laugh. He will never ridicule others, but will accept ridicule when it is deserved and laugh it off when it's not. He will not demean another for making a mistake, because he knows he may be the next to fail.

A professional understands his supreme arrogance, and that the fates will eventually notice and level their aim. When that aim connects, the best you can do is take Howard's advice: Laugh.

BIBLIOGRAPHY

[**PPP2001**]: Robert C. Martin, *Principles, Patterns, and Practices of Agile Software Development,* Upper Saddle River, NJ: Prentice Hall, 2002.

SAYING 2 NO

"Do; or do not. There is no trying."

— *Yoda*

In the early '70s, I, and two of my nineteen-year-old friends were working on a real-time accounting system for the Teamster's union in Chicago for a company named ASC. If names like Jimmy Hoffa come to mind, they should. You didn't mess around with the teamsters in 1971.

Our system was supposed to go live by a certain date. A *lot* of money was riding on that date. Our team had been working 60-, 70-, and 80-hour weeks to try to hold to that schedule.

A week before the go-live date we finally got the system put together in its entirety. There were lots of bugs and issues to deal with, and we frantically worked through the list. There was barely time to eat and sleep, let alone think.

Frank, the manager of ASC, was a retired Air Force colonel. He was one of those loud, in-your-face kind of managers. It was his way or the highway, and he'd put you on that highway by dropping you from 10,000 feet without a parachute. We nineteen year olds were barely able to make eye contact with him.

Frank said it had to be done by the date. That was all there was to it. The date would come, and we would be done. Period. No discussion. Over and out.

My boss, Bill, was a likeable guy. He'd been working with Frank for quite a few years and understood what was possible with Frank, and what was not. He told us that we were going live on the date, no matter what.

So we went live on the date. And it was a blazing disaster.

There were a dozen 300-baud, half-duplex terminals that connected Teamster's headquarters in Chicago to our machine thirty miles north in the suburbs. Each of those terminals locked up every 30 minutes or so. We had seen this problem before but had not simulated the traffic that the union data-entry clerks were suddenly slamming into our system.

To make matters worse, the tear sheets being printed on the ASR35 teletypes that were also connected to our system by 110-baud phone lines would freeze up in the middle of printing.

The solution to these freeze-ups was to reboot. So they'd have to get everybody whose terminal was still live to finish their work and then stop. When everyone was stopped, then they'd call us to reboot. The people who had been frozen would have to start over. And this was happening more than once per hour.

After half a day of this, the Teamster's office manager told us to shut the system down and not bring it up again until we had it working. Meanwhile, they had lost a half day of work and were going to have to re-enter it all using the old system.

We heard Frank's wails and roars all through the building. They went on for a long, long time. Then Bill, and our system's analyst Jalil, came to us and asked when we could have the system stable. I said, "four weeks."

The look on their faces was horror and then determination. "No," they said, "it must be running by Friday."

So I said, "Look, we just barely got this system to sort-of work last week. We need to shake down the troubles and issues. We need four weeks."

But Bill and Jalil were adamant. "No, it's really got to be Friday. Can you at least try?"

Then our team leader said, "OK, we'll try."

Friday was a good choice, The weekend load was a lot lower. We were able to find more problems and correct them before Monday came. Even so, the whole house of cards nearly came tumbling down again. The freeze-up problems kept on happening once or twice a day. There were other problems too. But gradually, after a few more weeks, we got the system to the point where the complaints died down, and normal life looked like it might actually be possible.

And then, as I told you in the introduction, we all quit. And they were left with a real crisis on their hands. They had to hire a new batch of programmers to try to deal with the huge stream of issues coming from the customer.

Who can we blame this debacle on? Clearly, Frank's style is part of the problem. His intimidations made it difficult for him to hear the truth. Certainly Bill and Jalil should have pushed back on Frank much harder than they did. Certainly our team lead should not have caved in to the Friday demand. And certainly I should have continued to say "no" instead of getting in line behind our team lead.

Professionals speak truth to power. Professionals have the courage to say no to their managers.

How do you say no to your boss? After all, it's your *boss!* Aren't you supposed to do what your boss says?

No. Not if you are a professional.

Slaves are not allowed to say no. Laborers may be hesitant to say no. But professionals are *expected* to say no. Indeed, good managers crave someone who has the guts to say no. It's the only way you can really get anything done.

ADVERSARIAL ROLES

One of the reviewers of this book truly hated this chapter. He said that it almost made him put the book down. He had built teams where there were no adversarial relationships; the teams worked together in harmony and without confrontation.

I'm happy for this reviewer, but I wonder if his teams are really as confrontation free as he supposes. And if they are, I wonder if they are as efficient as they could be. My own experience has been that the hard decisions are best made through the confrontation of adversarial roles.

Managers are people with a job to do, and most managers know how to do that job pretty well. Part of that job is to pursue and defend their objectives as aggressively as they can.

By the same token, programmers are also people with a job to do, and most of them know how to get that job done pretty well. If they are professionals they will pursue and defend *their* objectives as aggressively as *they* can.

When your manager tells you that the login page has to be ready by tomorrow, he is pursuing and defending one of his objectives. He's doing his job. If you know full well that getting the login page done by tomorrow is impossible, then you are not doing your job if you say "OK, I'll try." The only way to do your job, at that point, is to say "No, that's impossible."

But don't you have to do what your manager says? No, your manager is counting on you to defend your objectives as aggressively as he defends his. That's how the two of you are going to get to *the best possible outcome.*

The best possible outcome is the goal that you and your manager share. The trick is to find that goal, and that usually takes negotiation.

Negotiation can sometimes be pleasant.

> Mike: "Paula, I need the login page done by tomorrow."
> Paula: "Oh, wow! That soon? Well, OK, I'll try."
> Mike: "OK, that's great. Thanks!"

That was a nice little conversation. All confrontation was avoided. Both parties left smiling. Nice.

But both parties were behaving unprofessionally. Paula knows full well that the login page is going to take her longer than a day, so she's just lying. She might not think of it as a lie. Perhaps she thinks she *actually will try*, and maybe she holds out some meager hope that she'll actually get it done. But in the end, it's still a lie.

Mike, on the other hand, accepted the "I'll try" as "Yes." That's just a dumb thing to do. He should have known that Paula was trying to avoid confrontation, so he should have pressed the issue by saying, "You seem hesitant. Are you sure you can get it done tomorrow?"

Here's another pleasant conversation.

> Mike: "Paula, I need the login page done by tomorrow."
> Paula: "Oh, sorry Mike, but it's going to take me more time than that."
> Mike: "When do you think you can have it done?"
> Paula: "How about two weeks from now?"
> Mike: (scribbles something in his daytimer) "OK, thanks."

As pleasant as that was, it was also terribly dysfunctional and utterly unprofessional. Both parties failed in their search for the best possible outcome. Instead of asking whether two weeks would be OK, Paula should have been more assertive: "It's going to take me two weeks, Mike."

Mike, on the other hand, just accepted the date without question, as though his own objectives didn't matter. One wonders if he's not going to simply report back to his boss that the customer demo will have to be postponed because of Paula. That kind of passive-aggressive behavior is morally reprehensible.

In all these cases neither party has pursued a common acceptable goal. Neither party has been looking for the best possible outcome. Let's try this.

Mike: "Paula, I need the login page done by tomorrow."

Paula: "No, Mike, that's a two-week job."

Mike: "Two weeks? The architects estimated it at three days and it's already been five!"

Paula: "The architects were wrong, Mike. They did their estimates before product marketing got hold of the requirements. I've got at least ten more days of work to do on this. Didn't you see my updated estimate on the wiki?"

Mike: (looking stern and trembling with frustration) "This isn't acceptable Paula. Customers are coming for a demo tomorrow, and I've got to show them the login page working."

Paula: "What part of the login page do you need working by tomorrow?"

Mike: "I need *the login page!* I need to be able to *log in.*"

Paula: "Mike, I can give you a mock-up of the login page that will let you log in. I've got that working now. It won't actually check your username and password, and it won't email a forgotten password to you. It won't have the company news banner "Times-squaring" around the top of it, and the help button and hover text won't work. It won't store a cookie to remember you for next time, and it won't put any permission restrictions on you. But you'll be able to log in. Will that do?"

Mike: "I'll be able to log in?"

Paula: "Yes, you'll be able to log in."

Mike: "That's great Paula, you're a life saver!" (walks away pumping the air and saying "Yes!")

They reached the best possible outcome. They did this by saying no and then working out a solution that was mutually agreeable to both. They were acting like professionals. The conversation was a bit adversarial, and there were a few uncomfortable moments, but that's to be expected when two people assertively pursue goals that aren't in perfect alignment.

WHAT ABOUT THE WHY?

Perhaps you think that Paula should have explained *why* the login page was going to take so much longer. My experience is that the *why* is a lot less important than the *fact*. That fact is that the login page will require two weeks. Why it will take two weeks is just a detail.

Still, knowing why might help Mike to understand, and therefore to accept, the fact. Fair enough. And in situations where Mike has the technical expertise and temperament to understand, such explanations might be useful. On the other hand, Mike might disagree with the conclusion. Mike might decide that Paula was doing it all wrong. He might tell her that she doesn't need all that testing, or all that reviewing, or that step 12 could be omitted. Providing too much detail can be an invitation for micro-management.

HIGH STAKES

The most important time to say no is when the stakes are highest. The higher the stakes, the more valuable no becomes.

This should be self-evident. When the cost of failure is so high that the survival of your company depends upon it, you must be absolutely determined to give your managers the best information you can. And that often means saying no.

> Don (Director of Development): "So, our current estimate for completion of the Golden Goose project is twelve weeks from today, with an uncertainty of plus or minus five weeks."
>
> Charles (CEO): (sits glaring for fifteen seconds as his face reddens) "Do you mean to sit there and tell me that we might be seventeen weeks from delivery?"

Don: "That's possible, yes."

Charles: (stands up, Don stands up a second later) "Damm it Don! This
           was supposed to be done three weeks ago! I've got Galitron
           calling me every day wondering where their frakking system is.
           I am *not* going to tell them that they have to wait another four
           months? You've got to do better."

Don: Chuck, I told you *three months ago*, after all the layoffs, that we'd
           need four more months. I mean, Christ Chuck, you cut my staff
           twenty percent! Did you tell Galitron then that we'd be late?"

Charles: "You know damned well I didn't. We can't afford to lose that order
           Don. (Charles pauses, his face goes white) Without Galitron, we're
           really hosed. You know that, don't you? And now with this delay,
           I'm afraid . . . What will I tell the board? (He slowly sits back down
           in his seat, trying not to crumble.) Don, you've got to do better."

Don: "There's nothing I can do Chuck. We've been through this already.
           Galitron won't cut scope, and they won't accept any interim
           releases. They want to do the installation once and be done with
           it. I simply cannot do that any faster. It's *not* going to happen."

Charles: "Damn. I don't suppose it would matter if I told you your job
           was at stake."

Don: "Firing me isn't going to change the estimate, Charles."

Charles: "We're done here. Go back to your team and keep this project
           moving. I've got some very tough phone calls to make."

Of course, Charles should have told Galitron no three months ago when he first
found out about the new estimate. At least now he's doing the right thing by
calling them (and the board). But if Don hadn't stuck to his guns, those calls
might have been delayed even longer.

BEING A "TEAM PLAYER"

We've all heard how important it is to be a "team player." Being a team player
means playing your position as well as you possibly can, and helping out your
teammates when they get into a jam. A team-player communicates frequently,
keeps an eye out for his or her teammates, and executes his or her own
responsibilities as well as possible.

A team player is not someone who says yes all the time. Consider this scenario:

Paula: "Mike, I've got those estimates for you. The team agrees that we'll be ready to give a demo in about eight weeks, give or take one week."

Mike: "Paula, we've already scheduled the demo for six weeks from now."

Paula: "Without hearing from us first? Come on Mike, you can't push that on us."

Mike: "It's already done."

Paula: (sigh) "OK, look, I'll go back to the team and find out what we can safely deliver in six weeks, but it won't be the whole system. There'll be some features missing, and the data load will be incomplete."

Mike: "Paula, the customer is expecting to see a complete demo."

Paula: "That's not going to happen Mike."

Mike: "Damn. OK, work up the best plan you can and let me know tomorrow."

Paula: "That I can do."

Mike: "Isn't there something you can do to bring this date in? Maybe there's a way to work smarter and get creative."

Paula: "We're all pretty creative, Mike. We've got a good handle on the problem, and the date is going to be eight or nine weeks, not six."

Mike: "You could work overtime."

Paula: "That just makes us go slower, Mike. Remember the mess we made last time we mandated overtime?"

Mike: "Yeah, but that doesn't have to happen this time."

Paula: "It'll be just like last time, Mike. Trust me. It's going to be eight or nine weeks, not six."

Mike: "OK, get me your best plan, but keep thinking about how to get it done in six weeks. I know you guys'll figure out something."

Paula: "No, Mike, we won't. I'll get you a plan for six weeks, but it will be missing a lot of features and data. That's just how it's going to be."

Mike: "OK, Paula, but I bet you guys can work miracles if you try."

(Paula walks away shaking her head.)

Later, in the Director's strategy meeting ...

Don: "OK Mike, as you know the customer is coming in for a demo in six weeks. They're expecting to see everything working."

Mike: "Yes, and we'll be ready. My team is busting their butts on this and we're going to get it done. We'll have to work some overtime, and get pretty creative, but we'll make it happen!"

Don: "It's great that you and your staff are such team players."

Who were the *real* team players in this scenario? Paula was playing for the team, because she represented what could, and could not, be done to the best of her ability. She aggressively defended her position, despite the wheedling and cajoling from Mike. Mike was playing on a team of one. Mike is for Mike. He's clearly not on Paula's team because he just committed her to something she explicitly said she couldn't do. He's not on Don's team either (though he'd disagree) because he just lied through his teeth.

So why did Mike do this? He wanted Don to see him as a team player, and he has faith in his ability to wheedle and manipulate Paula into *trying* for the six-week deadline. Mike is not evil; he's just too confident in his ability to get people to do what he wants.

TRYING

The worst thing Paula could do in response to Mike's manipulations is say "OK, we'll try." I hate to channel Yoda here, but in this instance he is correct. *There is no trying.*

Perhaps you don't like that idea? Perhaps you think *trying* is a positive thing to do. After all, would Columbus have discovered America if he hadn't tried?

The word *try* has many definitions. The definition I take issue with here is "to apply extra effort." What extra effort could Paula apply to get the demo ready in time? If there *is* extra effort she could apply, then she and her team must not have been applying all their effort before. They must have been holding some effort in reserve.[1]

---

1. Like Foghorn Leghorn: "I always keep my feathers numbered for just such an emergency."

The promise to try is an admission that you've been holding back, that you have a reservoir of extra effort that you can apply. The promise to try is an admission that the goal is attainable through the application of this extra effort; moreover, it is a commitment to apply that extra effort to achieve the goal. Therefore, by promising to try you are committing to succeed. This puts the burden on you. If your "trying" does not lead to the desired outcome, you will have failed.

Do you have an extra reservoir of energy that you've been holding back? If you apply these reserves, will you be able to meet the goal? Or, by promising to try are you simply setting yourself up for failure?

By promising to try you are promising to change your plans. After all, the plans you had were insufficient. By promising to try you are saying that you have a new plan. What is that new plan? What change will you make to your behavior? What different things are you going to do because now you are "trying"?

If you don't have a new plan, if you don't make a change to your behavior, if you do everything exactly as you would have before you promised to "try," then what does trying mean?

If you are not holding back some energy in reserve, if you don't have a new plan, if you aren't going to change your behavior, and if you are reasonably confident in your original estimate, then promising to try is fundamentally dishonest. You are *lying*. And you are probably doing it to save face and to avoid a confrontation.

Paula's approach was much better. She continued to remind Mike that the team's estimate was uncertain. She always said "eight or nine weeks." She stressed the uncertainty and never backed off. She never suggested that there might be some extra effort, or some new plan, or some change in behavior that could reduce that uncertainty.

Three weeks later …

> Mike: "Paula, the demo is in three weeks, and the customers are demanding to see FILE UPLOAD working."
> Paula: "Mike, that's not on the list of features we agreed to."

Mike: "I know, but they're demanding it."

Paula: "OK, that means that either SINGLE SIGN-ON or BACKUP will have to be dropped from the demo."

Mike: "Absolutely not! They're expecting to see those features working as well!"

Paula: "So then, they are expecting to see every feature working. Is that what you are telling me? I told you that wasn't going to happen."

Mike: "I'm sorry Paula, but the customer just won't budge on this. They want to see it all."

Paula: "That's not going to happen, Mike. It's just not."

Mike: "Come on Paula, can't you guys at least *try*?"

Paula: "Mike, I could *try* to levitate. I could *try* to change lead in to gold. I could *try* to swim across the Atlantic. Do you think I'd succeed?"

Mike: "Now you're being unreasonable. I'm not asking for the *impossible*."

Paula: "Yes, Mike, you *are*."

(Mike smirks, nods, and turns to walk away.)

Mike: "I've got faith in you Paula; I know you won't let me down."

Paula: (speaking to Mike's back) "Mike, you're dreaming. This *is not* going to end well."

(Mike just waves without turning around.)

PASSIVE AGGRESSION

Paula's got an interesting decision to make. She suspects that Mike is not telling Don about her estimates. She could just let Mike walk off the end of the cliff. She could make sure that copies of all the appropriate memos were on file, so that when the disaster strikes she can show *what* she told Mike, and *when* she told him. This is passive aggression. She'd just let Mike hang himself.

Or, she could try to head off the disaster by communicating directly with Don. This is risky, to be sure, but it's also what being a team player is really all about. When a freight train is bearing down on you and you are the only one who can see it, you can either step quietly off the track and watch everyone else get run over, or you can yell "Train! Get off the track!"

Two days later ...

Paula: "Mike, have you told Don about my estimates? Has he told the customer that the demo will not have the FILE UPLOAD feature working?"

Mike: "Paula, you said you'd get that working for me."

Paula: "No, Mike, I didn't. I told you that it was impossible. Here's a copy of the memo I sent you after our talk."

Mike: "Yeah, but you were going to *try* anyway, right?"

Paula: "We've already had that discussion Mike. Remember, gold and lead?"

Mike: (sighs) "Look, Paula, you've just got to do it. You just have to. Please do whatever it takes, but you just have to make this happen for me."

Paula: "Mike. You're wrong. I don't have to make this happen for you. What I *have* to do, if you don't, is tell Don."

Mike: "That'd be going over my head, you wouldn't do that."

Paula: "I don't want to Mike, but I will if you force me."

Mike: "Oh, Paula . . ."

Paula: "Look, Mike, the features *aren't* going to get done in time for the demo. You need to get this into your head. Stop trying to convince me to work harder. Stop deluding yourself that I'm somehow going to pull a rabbit out of a hat. Face the fact that you have to tell Don, and you have to tell him *today*."

Mike: (Eyes wide) "Today?"

Paula: "Yes, Mike. Today. Because tomorrow I expect to have a meeting with you and Don about which features to include in the demo. If that meeting doesn't happen tomorrow, then I will be forced to go to Don myself. Here's a copy of the memo that explains just that."

Mike: "You're just covering your ass!"

Paula: "Mike, I'm trying to cover *both* our asses. Can you imagine the debacle if the customer comes here expecting a full demo and we can't deliver?"

What happens in the end to Paula and Mike? I'll leave it to you to work out the possibilities. The point is that Paula has behaved very professionally. She has said no at all the right times, and in all the right ways. She said no when pushed to amend her estimates. She said no when manipulated, cajoled, and begged. And, most importantly, she said no to Mike's self-delusion and inaction. Paula was playing for the team. Mike needed help, and she used every means in her power to help him.

THE COST OF SAYING YES

Most of the time we want to say yes. Indeed, healthy teams strive to find a way to say yes. Manager and developers in well-run teams will negotiate with each other until they come to a mutually agreed upon plan of action.

But, as we've seen, sometimes the only way to get to the *right* yes is to be unafraid so say no.

Consider the following story that John Blanco posted on his blog.[2] It is reprinted here with permission. As you read it, ask yourself when and how he should have said no.

IS GOOD CODE IMPOSSIBLE?

When you hit your teenage years you decide you want to be a software developer. During your high school years, you learn how to write software using object-oriented principles. When you graduate to college, you apply all the principles you've learned to areas such as artificial intelligence or 3D graphics.

And when you hit the professional circuit, you begin your never-ending quest to write commercial-quality, maintainable, and "perfect" code that will stand the test of time.

Commercial quality. Huh. That's pretty funny.

I consider myself lucky, I *love* design patterns. I like studying the theory of coding perfection. I have no problem starting up an hour-long discussion about why my XP partner's choice of inheritance hierarchy is wrong—that HAS-A is better than IS-A in so many cases. But something has been bugging me lately and I am wondering something . . .

. . . Is good code impossible in modern software development?

---

2. http://raptureinvenice.com/?p=63

The Typical Project Proposal

As a full-time contract developer (and part-time), I spend my days (and nights) developing mobile applications for clients. And what I've learned over the many years I've been doing this is that the demands of client work preclude me from writing the real quality apps that I'd like.

Before I begin, let me just say it's not for a lack of trying. I love the topic of clean code. I don't know anyone who pursues that perfect software design like I do. It's the execution that I find more elusive, and not for the reason you think.

Here, let me tell you a story.

Towards the end of last year, a fairly well-known company put out an RFP (Request for Proposal) to have an app built for them. They're a huge retailer, but for the sake of anonymity let's call them Gorilla Mart. They say they need to create an iPhone presence and would like an app produced for them by Black Friday. The catch? It's already November 1st. That leaves just under 4 weeks to create the app. Oh, and at this time Apple is still taking two weeks to approve apps. (Ah, the good old days.) So, wait, this app has to be written in . . . TWO WEEKS?!?!

Yes. We have two weeks to write this app. And, unfortunately, we've won the bid. (In business, client importance matters.) This is going to happen.

> "But it's OK," Gorilla Mart Executive #1 says. "The app is simple. It just needs to show users a few products from our catalog and let them search for store locations. We already do it on our site. We'll give you the graphics, too. You can probably—what's the word—yeah, hardcode it!"

> Gorilla Mart Executive #2 chimes in. "And we just need a couple of coupons the user can show at the cash register. The app will be a throwaway. Let's get it out the door, and then for Phase II we'll do something bigger and better from scratch."

And then it's happening. Despite years of constant reminders that every feature a client asks for will always be more complex to write than it is to explain, you go for it. You really believe that this time it really can be done in two weeks. Yes! We can do this! This time it's different! It's just a few graphics and a service call to get a store location. XML! No sweat. We can do this. I'm pumped! Let's go!

It takes just a day for you and reality to once again make acquaintance.

> Me: So, can you give me the info I need to call your store location web service?

> The Client: What's a web service?

> Me: . . . .

Continues

And that's exactly how it happened. Their store location service, found right where it's supposed to be on the top-right corner of their web site, is not a web service. It's generated by Java code. Ix-nay with the API-ay. And to boot, it's hosted by a Gorilla Mart strategic partner.

Enter the nefarious "3rd party."

In client terms, a "3rd party" is akin to Angelina Jolie. Despite the promise that you'll be able to have an enlightening conversation over a nice meal and hopefully hook up afterwards … sorry, it ain't happenin'. You're just gonna have to fantasize about it while you take care of business yourself.

In my case, the only thing I was able to wrestle out of Gorilla Mart was a current snapshot of their current store listings in an Excel file. I had to write the store location search code from scratch.

The double-whammy came later that day: They wanted the product and coupon data online so it could be changed weekly. There goes hardcoding! Two weeks to write an iPhone app have now become two weeks to write an iPhone app, a PHP backend, and integrate them togeth— … What? They want me to handle QA, too?

To make up for the extra work, the coding will have to go a little faster. Forget that abstract factory. Use a big fat for loop instead of the composite, there's no time!

Good code has become impossible.

Two Weeks to Completion

Let me tell you, that two weeks was pretty miserable. First, two of the days were eliminated due to all-day meetings for my next project. (That amplifies how short a time frame this was going to be.) Ultimately, I really had eight days to get things done. The first week I worked 74 hours and the next week … God … I don't even recall, it's been eradicated from my synapses. Probably a good thing.

I spent those eight days writing code in a fury. I used all the tools available to me to get it done: copy and paste (AKA reusable code), magic numbers (avoiding the duplication of defining constants and then, gasp!, retyping them), and absolutely NO unit tests! (Who needs red bars at a time like this, it'd just demotivate me!)

It was pretty bad code and I never had time to refactor. Considering the time frame, however, it was actually pretty stellar, and it was "throwaway" code after all, right? Does any of this sound familiar? Well just wait, it gets better.

As I was putting the final touches on the app (the final touches being writing the entirety of the server code), I started to look at the codebase and wondered if maybe it was worth it. The app was done after all. I survived!

"Hey, we just hired Bob, and he's very busy and he couldn't make the call, but he says we should be requiring users to provide their email addresses to get the coupons. He hasn't seen the app, but he thinks this would be a great idea! We also want a reporting system to get those emails from the server. One that's nice and not too expensive. (Wait, that last part was Monty Python.) Speaking of coupons, they need to be able to expire after a number of days we specify. Oh, and …"

Let's step back. What do we know about what good code is? Good code should be extendable. Maintainable. It should lend itself to modification. It should read like prose. Well, this wasn't good code.

Another thing. If you want to be a better developer, you must always keep this inevitably in mind: The client will always extend the deadline. They will always want more features. They will always want change—LATE. And here's the formula for what to expect:

(# of Executives)^2
+ 2 * # of New Executives
+ # of Bob's Kids
= DAYS ADDED AT LAST MINUTE

Now, executives are decent people. I think. They provide for their family (assuming Satan has approved of their having one). They want the app to succeed (promotion time!). The problem is that they all want a direct claim to the project's success. When all is said and done, they all want to point at some feature or design decision they can each call their very own.

So, back to the story, we added a couple more days to the project and got the email feature done. And then I collapsed from exhaustion.

The Clients Never Care as Much as You Do

The clients, despite their protestations, despite their apparent urgency, never care as much as you do about the app being on time. The afternoon that I dubbed the app completed, I sent an email with the final build to all the stakeholders, Executives (hiss!), managers, and so on. "IT IS DONE! I BRING YOU V1.0! PRAISE THY NAME." I hit Send, lay back in my chair, and with a smug grin began to fantasize how the company would run me up onto their shoulders and lead a procession down 42nd Street while I was crowned "Greatest Developer Ev-ar." At the very least, my face would be on all their advertising, right?

Funny, they didn't seem to agree. In fact, I wasn't sure what they thought. I heard nothing. Not a peep. Turns out, the folks at Gorilla Mart were eager to and had already moved on to the next thing.

You think I lie? Check this out. I pushed to the Apple store without filling in an app description. I had requested one from Gorilla Mart, and they hadn't gotten back to me and there was no time to wait. (See previous paragraph.) I wrote them again. And again. I got

Continues

some of our own management on it. Twice I heard back and twice I was told, "What did you need again?" I NEED THE APP DESCRIPTION!

One week later, Apple started testing the app. This is usually a time of joyousness, but it was instead a time for mortal dread. As expected, later in the day the app was rejected. It was about the saddest, poorest excuse to allow a rejection I can imagine: "App is missing an app description." Functionally perfect; no app description. And for this reason Gorilla Mart didn't have their app ready for Black Friday. I was pretty upset.

I'd sacrificed my family for a two-week super sprint, and no one at Gorilla Mart could be bothered to create an app description given a week of time. They gave it to us an hour after the rejection—apparently that was the signal to get down to business.

If I was upset before, I would become livid a week and a half after that. You see, they still hadn't gotten us real data. The products and coupons on the server were fake. Imaginary. The coupon code was 1234567890. You know, phoney baloney. (Bologna is spelled baloney when used in that context, BTW.)

And it was that fateful morning that I checked the Portal and THE APP WAS AVAILABLE! Fake data and all! I cried out in abject horror and called up whoever I could and screamed, "I NEED THE DATA!" and the woman on the other end asked me if I needed fire or police, so I hung up on 911. But then I called Gorilla Mart and was like, "I NEED DATA!" And I'll never forget the response:

> Oh, hey there John. We have a new VP and we've decided not to release. Pull it off the App Store, would you?

In the end, it turned out that at least 11 people registered their email addresses in the database, which meant there were 11 people that could potentially walk into a Gorilla Mart with a fake iPhone coupon in tow. Boy, that might get ugly.

When it was all said and done, the client had said one thing correctly all along: The code was a throwaway. The only problem is, it was never released in the first place.

Result? Rush to Complete, Slow to Market

The lesson in the story is that your stakeholders, whether an external client or internal management, have figured out how to get developers to write code quickly. Effectively? No. Quickly? Yes. Here's how it works:

- **Tell the developer the app is simple.** This serves to pressure the development team into a false frame of mind. It also gets the developers to start working earlier, whereby they …

- **Add features by faulting the team for not recognizing their necessity.** In this case, the hardcoded content was going to require app updates to change. How could I not realize that? I did, but I'd been handed a false promise earlier, that's why. Or a client will hire "a new guy" who's recognized there is some obvious omission. One day a client will say they just hired Steve Jobs and can we add alchemy to the app? Then they'll …

- **Push the deadline. Over and over.** Developers work their fastest and hardest (and BTW are at their most error prone, but who cares about that, right?) with a couple days to go on a deadline. Why tell them you can push the date out further while they're being so productive? Take advantage of it! And so it goes, a few days are added, a week is added, just when you had worked a 20-hour shift to get everything just right. It's like a donkey and carrot, except you're not treated as well as the donkey.

It's a brilliant playbook. Can you blame them for thinking it works? But they don't see the God-awful code. And so it happens, time and again, despite the results.

In a globalized economy, where corporations are held to the almighty dollar and raising the stock price involves layoffs, overworked staffs, and offshoring, this strategy I've shown you of cutting developer costs is making good code obsolete. As developers, we're going to be asked/told/conned into writing twice the code in half the time if we're not careful.

CODE IMPOSSIBLE

In the story when John asks "Is good code impossible?", he is really asking "Is professionalism impossible?" After all, it wasn't just the code that suffered in his tale of dysfunction. It was his family, his employer, his customer, and the users. *Everybody* lost[3] in this adventure. And they lost due to unprofessionalism.

So who was acting unprofessionally? John makes it clear that he thinks it was the executives at Gorilla Mart. After all, his playbook was a pretty clear indictment of their bad behavior. But *was* their behavior bad? I don't think so.

---

3. With the possible exception of John's direct employer, though I'd bet they lost too.

The folks at Gorilla Mart wanted the option to have an iPhone app on Black Friday. They were willing to pay to have that option. They found someone willing to provide that option. So how can you fault them?

Yes, it's true, there were some communications failures. Apparently the executives didn't know what a web service really was, and there were all the normal issues of one part of a big corporation not knowing what another part is doing. But all that should have been expected. John even admits as much when he says: "Despite years of constant reminders that every feature a client asks for will always be more complex to write than it is to explain . . ."

So if the culprit was not Gorilla Mart, then who?

Perhaps it was John's direct employer. John didn't say this explicitly, but there was a hint when he said, parenthetically, "In business, client importance matters." So did John's employer make unreasonable promises to Gorilla Mart? Did they put pressure on John, directly or indirectly, to make those promises come true? John doesn't say this, so we can only wonder.

Even so, where is John's responsibility in all of this? I put the fault squarely on John. John is the one who accepted the initial two-week deadline, knowing full well that projects are usually more complex than they sound. John is the one who accepted the need to write the PHP server. John is the one who accepted the email registration, and the coupon expiration. John is the one who worked 20-hour days and 90-hour weeks. John is the one who subtracted himself from his family and his life to make this deadline.

And why did John do this? He tells us in no uncertain terms: "I hit Send, lay back in my chair, and with a smug grin began to fantasize how the company would run me up onto their shoulders and lead a procession down 42nd Street while I was crowned "Greatest Developer Ev-ar." In short, John was trying to be a hero. He saw his chance for accolades, and he went for it. He leaned over and grabbed for the brass ring.

Professionals are often heroes, but not because they try to be. Professionals become heroes when they get a job done well, on time, and on budget. By trying to become the man of the hour, the savior of the day, John was not acting like a professional.

John should have said no to the original two-week deadline. Or if not, then he should have said no when he found there was no web service. He should have said no to the request for email registration and coupon expiration. He should have said no to anything that would require horrific overtime and sacrifice.

But most of all, John should have said no to his own internal decision that the only way to get this job done on time was to make a big mess. Notice what John said about good code and unit tests:

"To make up for the extra work, the coding will have to go a little faster. Forget that abstract factory. Use a big fat for loop instead of the composite, there's no time!"

And again:

"I spent those eight days writing code in a fury. I used all the tools available to me to get it done: copy-and-paste (AKA reusable code), magic numbers (avoiding the duplication of defining constants and then, gasp!, retyping them), and absolutely NO unit tests! (Who needs red bars at a time like this, it'd just demotivate me!)"

Saying yes to those decisions was the real crux of the failure. John accepted that the only way to succeed was to behave unprofessionally, so he reaped the appropriate reward.

That may sound harsh. It's not intended that way. In previous chapters I described how I've made the same mistake in my career, more than once. The temptation to be a hero and "solve the problem" is huge. What we all have to realize is that saying yes to dropping our professional disciplines is *not* the way to solve problems. Dropping those disciplines is the way you create problems.

With that, I can finally answer John's initial question:

"Is good code impossible? Is professionalism impossible?"

Answer: I say *no*.

SAYING **3** YES

Did you know that I invented voice mail? It's true. Actually there were three of us who held the patent for voice mail. Ken Finder, Jerry Fitzpatrick, and I. It was in the very early 80s, and we worked for a company named Teradyne. Our CEO had commissioned us to come up with a new kind of product, and we invented "The Electronic Receptionist," or ER for short.

You all know what ER is. ER is one of those horrible machines that answers the phone at companies and asks you all kinds of brain-dead questions that you need to answer by pressing buttons. ("For English, press 1.")

Our ER would answer the phone for a company and ask you to dial the name of the person you wanted. It would ask you to pronounce your name, and then it would call the person in question. It would announce the call and ask whether it should be accepted. If so, it would connect the call and drop off.

You could tell ER where you were. You could give it several phone numbers to try. So if you were in someone else's office, ER could find you. If you were at home, ER could find you. If you were in a different city, ER could find you. And, in the end, if ER could not find you, it would take a message. That's where the voice mail came in.

Oddly enough, Teradyne could not figure out how to sell ER. The project ran out of budget and was morphed into something we knew how to sell—CDS, The Craft Dispatch System, for dispatching telephone repairmen to their next job. And Teradyne also dropped the patent without telling us. (!) The current patent holder filed three months after we did. (!!)[1]

Long after the morphing of ER into CDS, but long before I found out that the patent had been dropped. I waited in a tree for the CEO of the company. We had a big oak tree outside the front of the building. I climbed it and waited for his Jaguar to pull in. I met him at the door and asked for a few minutes. He obliged.

I told him we really needed to start up the ER project again. I told him I was sure it could make money. He surprised me by saying, "OK Bob, work up a plan. Show me how I can make money. If you do, and I believe it, I'll start up ER again."

I hadn't expected that. I had expected him to say, "You're right Bob. I'm going to start that project up again, and I'm going to figure out how to make money at

---

1. Not that the patent was worth any money to me. I had sold it to Teradyne for $1, as per my employment contract (and I didn't get the dollar).

it." But no. He put the burden back on me. And it was a burden I was ambivalent about. After all, I was a software guy, not a money guy. I wanted to work on the ER project, not be responsible for profit and loss. But I didn't want to show my ambivalence. So I thanked him and left his office with these words:

"Thanks Russ. I'm committed . . . I guess."

With that, let me introduce you to Roy Osherove, who will tell you just how pathetic that statement was.

A LANGUAGE OF COMMITMENT

By Roy Osherove

Say. Mean. Do.

There are three parts to making a commitment.

1. You *say* you'll do it.
2. You *mean* it.
3. You *actually do* it.

But how often do we encounter other people (not ourselves, of course!) who never go all the way with these three stages?

- **You ask the IT guy** why the network is so slow and he says "Yeah. We really need to get some new routers." And you *know* nothing will ever happen in that category.
- **You ask a team member** to run some manual tests before checking in the source code, and he replies, "Sure. I hope to get to it by the end of the day." And somehow you *feel* that you'll need to ask tomorrow if any testing really took place before check-in.
- **Your boss** wanders into the room and mumbles, "we have to move faster." And you *know* he really means YOU have to move faster. *He's* not going to do anything about it.

There are very few people who, when they say something, they mean it and then actually get it done. There are some who will say things and *mean* them, but they never get it done. And there are far more people who promise things and don't even *mean* to do them. Ever heard someone say, "Man, I really need to lose some weight," and you knew they are not going to do anything about it? It happens all the time.

Why do we keep getting that strange feeling that, most of the time, people aren't really committed to getting something done?

Worse, often our intuition can fail us. Sometimes we'd *like* to believe someone really means what they say when they really don't. We'd *like* to believe a developer when they say, pressed to the corner, that they can finish that two-week task in one week instead, but we shouldn't.

Instead of trusting our guts, we can use some language-related tricks to try and figure out if people really mean what they say. And by changing what we say, we can start taking care of steps 1 and 2 of the previous list on our own. When we *say* we will commit to something, and we need to *mean* it.

RECOGNIZING LACK OF COMMITMENT

We should look at the language we use when we *commit* to doing something, as the telltale sign of things to come. Actually, it's more a matter of looking for specific *words* in what we say. If you can't find those little magic words, chances are we don't mean what we say, or we may not believe it to be feasible.

Here are some examples of words and phrases to look for that are telltale signs of noncommitment:

- **Need\should.** "We need to get this done." "I need to lose weight." "Someone should make that happen."
- **Hope\wish.** "I hope to get this done by tomorrow." "I hope we can meet again some day." "I wish I had time for that." "I wish this computer was faster."
- **Let's.** (not followed by "I . . .") "Let's meet sometime." "Let's finish this thing."

As you start to look for these words you'll see that you start spotting them almost everywhere around you, and even in things you say to others.

You'll find we tend to be very busy not taking responsibility for things.

And that's *not* okay when you or someone else relies on those promises as part of the job. You've taken the first step, though—start recognizing lack of commitment around you, and in you.

We heard what noncommitment sounds like. How do we recognize real commitment?

WHAT DOES COMMITMENT SOUND LIKE?

What's common in the phrases of the previous section is that they either assume things are out of "my" hands or they don't take personal responsibility. In each of these cases, people behave as if they were *victims* of a situation instead of in control of it.

The real truth is that *you, personally,* ALWAYS have something that's under *your* control, so there is always *something* you can fully commit to doing.

The secret ingredient to recognizing real commitment is to look for sentences that sound like this: I will . . . by . . . (example: I will finish this by Tuesday.)

What's important about this sentence? *You're stating a fact about something YOU will do with a clear end time.* You're *not* talking about anyone else but yourself. You're talking about an *action* that you *will* take. You won't *"possibly"* take it, or *"might get to it"*; you *will* achieve it.

There is (technically) no way out of this verbal commitment. You said you'll do it and now only a binary result is possible—you either get it done, or you don't. If you don't get it done, people can hold you up to your promises. You will feel *bad* about not doing it. You will feel *awkward* telling someone about not having done it (if that someone heard you promise you will).

Scary, isn't it?

You're taking full responsibility for something, in front of an audience of at least one person. It's not just you standing in front of the mirror, or the computer screen. It's you, facing another human being, and saying you'll do it. That's the start of commitment. Putting yourself in the situation that forces you to do something.

You've changed the language you use to a language of commitment, and that will help you get through the next two stages: meaning it, and following through.

Here are a number of reasons you might not *mean* it, or follow through, with some solutions.

It wouldn't work because I rely on person X to get this done.

You can only commit to things that you have *full control* of. For example, if your goal is to finish a module that also depends on another team, you can't commit to finish the module with full integration with the other team. But you *can* commit to specific actions that will bring you to your target. You could:

- Sit down for an hour with Gary from the infrastructure team to understand your dependencies.
- Create an interface that abstracts your module's dependency from the other team's infrastructure.
- Meet at least three times this week with the build guy to make sure your changes work well in the company's build system.
- Create your own personal build that runs your integration tests for the module.

See the difference?

If the end goal depends on someone else, you should commit to specific actions that bring you closer to the end goal.

It wouldn't work because I don't really know if it can be done.

If it can't be done, you can still commit to actions that will bring you closer to the target. Finding out if it can be done can be one of the actions to commit to!

Instead of committing to fix all 25 remaining bugs before the release (which may not be possible), you can commit to these specific actions that bring you closer to that goal:

- Go through all 25 bugs and try to recreate them.
- Sit down with the QA who found each bug to see a repro of that bug.
- Spend all the time you have this week trying to fix each bug.

It wouldn't work because sometimes I just won't make it.

That happens. Something unexpected might happen, and that's life. But you still want to live up to expectations. In that case, it's time to change the expectations, *as soon as possible.*

If you can't make your commitment, the most important thing is to raise a red flag as soon as possible to whoever you committed to.

The earlier you raise the flag to all stakeholders, the more likely there will be time for the team to stop, reassess the current actions being taken, and decide if something can be done or changed (in terms of priorities, for example). By doing this, your commitment can still be fulfilled, or you can change to a different commitment.

Some examples are:

- If you set a meeting for noon at a cafe downtown with a colleague and you get stuck in traffic, you doubt you'll be able to follow through on your commitment to be there on time. You can call your colleague as soon as you realize you might be late, and let them know. Maybe you can find a closer place to meet, or perhaps postpone the meeting.

- If you committed to solving a bug you thought was solvable and you realize at some point the bug is much more hideous than previously thought, you can raise the flag. The team can then decide on a course of action to make that commitment (pairing, spiking on potential solutions, brainstorming) or change the priority and move you over to another simpler bug.

One important point here is: If you don't tell anyone about the potential problem as soon as possible, you're not giving anyone a chance to help you follow through on your commitment.

SUMMARY

Creating a language of commitment may sound a bit scary, but it can help solve many of the communication problems programmers face today—estimations, deadlines, and face-to-face communication mishaps. You'll be taken as a serious developer who lives up to their word, and that's one of the best things you can hope for in our industry.

~~~

LEARNING HOW TO SAY "YES"

I asked Roy to contribute that article because it struck a chord within me. I've been preaching about learning how to say no for some time. But it is just as important to learn how to say yes.

THE OTHER SIDE OF "TRY"

Let's imagine that Peter is responsible for some modifications to the rating engine. He's privately estimated that these modifications will take him five or six days. He also thinks that writing the documentation for the modifications will take a few hours. On Monday morning his manager, Marge, asks him for status.

Marge: "Peter, will you have the rating engine mods done by Friday?"
Peter: "I think that's doable."

Marge: "Will that include the documentation?"

Peter: "I'll try to get that done as well."

Perhaps Marge can't hear the dithering in Peter's statements, but he's certainly not making much of a commitment. Marge is asking questions that demand boolean answers but Peter's boolean responses are fuzzy.

Notice the abuse of the word try. In the last chapter we used the "extra effort" definition of try. Here, Peter is using the "maybe, maybe not" definition.

Peter would be better off responding like this:

Marge: "Peter, will you have the rating engine mods done by Friday?"

Peter: "Probably, but it might be Monday."

Marge: "Will that include the documentation?"

Peter: "The documentation will take me another few hours, so Monday is possible, but it might be as late as Tuesday."

In this case Peter's language is more honest. He is describing his own uncertainty to Marge. Marge may be able to deal with that uncertainty. On the other hand, she might not.

COMMITTING WITH DISCIPLINE

Marge: "Peter, I need a definite yes or no. Will you have the rating engine finished and documented by Friday?"

This is a perfectly fair question for Marge to ask. She's got a schedule to maintain, and she needs a binary answer about Friday. How should Peter respond?

Peter: "In that case, Marge, I'll have to say no. The soonest I can be *sure* that I'll be done with the mods and the docs is Tuesday."

Marge: "You are committing to Tuesday?"

Peter: "Yes, I will have it all ready on Tuesday."

But what if Marge really needs the modifications and documentation done by Friday?

> Marge: "Peter, Tuesday gives me a real problem. Willy, our tech writer, will be available on Monday. He's got five days to finish up the user guide. If I don't have the rating engine docs by Monday morning, he'll never get the manual done on time. Can you do the docs first?"

> Peter: "No, the mods have to come first, because we generate the docs from the output of the test runs."

> Marge: "Well, isn't there some way you can finish up the mods and the docs before Monday morning?"

Now Peter has a decision to make. There is a good chance he'll be done with the rate engine modifications on Friday, and he might even be able to finish up the docs before he goes home for the weekend. He *could* do a few hours of work on Saturday too if things take longer than he hopes. So what should he tell Marge?

> Peter: "Look Marge, there's a good chance that I can get everything done by Monday morning if I put in a few extra hours on Saturday."

Does that solve Marge's problem? No, it simply changes the odds, and that's what Peter needs to tell her.

> Marge: "Can I count on Monday morning then?"
> Peter: "Probably, but not definitely."

That might not be good enough for Marge.

> Marge: "Look, Peter, I really need a definite on this. Is there *any* way you can commit to get this done before Monday morning?"

Peter might be tempted to break discipline at this point. He might be able to get done faster if he doesn't write his tests. He might be able to get done faster if he doesn't refactor. He might be able to get done faster if he doesn't run the full regression suite.

This is where the professional draws the line. First of all, Peter is just wrong about his suppositions. He *won't* get done faster if he doesn't write his tests. He *won't* get done faster if he doesn't refactor. He *won't* get done faster if he omits the full regression suite. Years of experience have taught us that breaking disciplines only slows us down.

But secondly, as a professional he has a responsibility to maintain certain standards. His code needs to be tested, and needs to have tests. His code needs to be clean. And he has to be sure he hasn't broken anything else in the system.

Peter, as a professional, has already made a commitment to maintain these standards. All other commitments he makes should be subordinate to that. So this whole line of reasoning needs to aborted.

> Peter: "No, Marge, there's really no way I can be certain about any date before Tuesday. I'm sorry if that messes up your schedule, but it's just the reality we're faced with."
>
> Marge: "Damn. I was really counting on bringing this one in sooner. You're sure?"
>
> Peter: "I'm sure that it might be as late as Tuesday, yes."
>
> Marge: "OK, I guess I'll go talk to Willy to see if he can rearrange his schedule."

In this case Marge accepted Peter's answer and started hunting for other options. But what if all Marge's options have been exhausted? What if Peter were the last hope?

> Marge: "Peter, look, I know this is a huge imposition, but I really need you to find a way to get this all done by Monday morning. It's really critical. Isn't there something you can do?"

So now Peter starts to think about working some significant overtime, and probably most of the weekend. He needs to be very honest with himself about his stamina and reserves. It's easy to *say* you'll get a lot done on the weekends, it's a lot harder to actually muster enough energy to do high-quality work.

Professionals know their limits. They know how much overtime they can effectively apply, and they know what the cost will be.

In this case Peter feels pretty confident that a few extra hours during the week and some time on the weekend will be sufficient.

> Peter: "OK, Marge, I'll tell you what. I'll call home and clear some overtime with my family. If they are OK with it, then I'll get this task done by Monday morning. I'll even come in on Monday morning to make sure everything goes smoothly with Willy. But then I'll go home and won't be back until Wednesday. Deal?"

This is perfectly fair. Peter knows that he can get the modifications and documents done if he works the overtime. He also knows he'll be useless for a couple of days after that.

CONCLUSION

Professionals are not required to say yes to everything that is asked of them. However, they should work hard to find creative ways to make "yes" possible. When professionals say yes, they use the language of commitment so that there is no doubt about what they've promised.

Coding

4

In a previous book[1] I wrote a great deal about the structure and nature of *Clean Code*. This chapter discusses the *act* of coding, and the context that surrounds that act.

When I was 18 I could type reasonably well, but I had to look at the keys. I could not type blind. So one evening I spent a few long hours at an IBM 029 keypunch refusing to look at my fingers as I typed a program that I had written on several coding forms. I examined each card after I typed it and discarded those that were typed wrong.

---

1. [Martin09]

At first I typed quite a few in error. By the end of the evening I was typing them all with near perfection. I realized, during that long night, that typing blind is all about *confidence*. My fingers knew where the keys were, I just had to gain the confidence that I wasn't making a mistake. One of the things that helped with that confidence is that I could *feel* when I was making an error. By the end of the evening, if I made a mistake, I knew it almost instantly and simply ejected the card without looking at it.

Being able to sense your errors is really important. Not just in typing, but in everything. Having error-sense means that you very rapidly close the feedback loop and learn from your errors all the more quickly. I've studied, and mastered, several disciplines since that day on the 029. I've found that in each case that the key to mastery is confidence and error-sense.

This chapter describes my personal set of rules and principles for coding. These rules and principles are not about my code itself; they are about my behavior, mood, and attitude while writing code. They describe my own mental, moral, and emotional context for writing code. These are the roots of my confidence and error-sense.

You will likely not agree with everything I say here. After all, this is deeply personal stuff. In fact, you may violently disagree with some of my attitudes and principles. That's OK—they are not intended to be absolute truths for anyone other than me. What they are is one man's approach to being a professional coder.

Perhaps, by studying and contemplating my own personal coding milieu you can learn to snatch the pebble from my hand.

PREPAREDNESS

Coding is an intellectually challenging and exhausting activity. It requires a level of concentration and focus that few other disciplines require. The reason for this is that coding requires you to juggle many competing factors at once.

1. First, your code must work. You must understand what problem you are solving and understand how to solve that problem. You must ensure that the code you write is a faithful representation of that solution. You must manage

every detail of that solution while remaining consistent within the language, platform, current architecture, and all the warts of the current system.

2. Your code must solve the problem set for you by the customer. Often the customer's requirements do not actually solve the customer's problems. It is up to you to see this and negotiate with the customer to ensure that the customer's true needs are met.

3. Your code must fit well into the existing system. It should not increase the rigidity, fragility, or opacity of that system. The dependencies must be well-managed. In short, your code needs to follow solid engineering principles.[2]

4. Your code must be readable by other programmers. This is not simply a matter of writing nice comments. Rather, it requires that you craft the code in such a way that it reveals your intent. This is hard to do. Indeed, this may be the most difficult thing a programmer can master.

Juggling all these concerns is hard. It is physiologically difficult to maintain the necessary concentration and focus for long periods of time. Add to this the problems and distractions of working in a team, in an organization, and the cares and concerns of everyday life. The bottom line is that the opportunity for distraction is high.

When you cannot concentrate and focus sufficiently, the code you write will be wrong. It will have bugs. It will have the wrong structure. It will be opaque and convoluted. It will not solve the customers' real problems. In short, it will have to be reworked or redone. Working while distracted creates waste.

If you are tired or distracted, *do not code.* You'll only wind up redoing what you did. Instead, find a way to eliminate the distractions and settle your mind.

3 AM CODE

The worst code I ever wrote was at 3 AM. The year was 1988, and I was working at a telecommunications start-up named Clear Communications. We were all putting in long hours in order to build "sweat equity." We were, of course, all dreaming of being rich.

---

2. [Martin03]

One very late evening—or rather, one very early morning, in order to solve a timing problem—I had my code send a message to itself through the event dispatch system (we called this "sending mail"). This was the *wrong* solution, but at 3 AM it looked pretty damned good. Indeed, after 18 hours of solid coding (not to mention the 60–70 hour weeks) it was *all* I could think of.

I remember feeling so good about myself for the long hours I was working. I remember feeling *dedicated*. I remember thinking that working at 3 AM is what serious professionals do. How wrong I was!

That code came back to bite us over and over again. It instituted a faulty design structure that everyone used but consistently had to work around. It caused all kinds of strange timing errors and odd feedback loops. We'd get into infinite mail loops as one message caused another to be sent, and then another, infinitely. We never had time to rewrite this wad (so we thought) but we always seemed to have time to add another wart or patch to work around it. The cruft grew and grew, surrounding that 3 AM code with ever more baggage and side effects. Years later it had become a team joke. Whenever I was tired or frustrated they'd say, "Look out! Bob's about to send mail to himself!"

The moral of this story is: Don't write code when you are tired. Dedication and professionalism are more about discipline than hours. Make sure that your sleep, health, and lifestyle are tuned so that you can put in eight *good* hours per day.

WORRY CODE

Have you ever gotten into a big fight with your spouse or friend, and then tried to code? Did you notice that there was a background process running in your mind trying to resolve, or at least review the fight? Sometimes you can feel the stress of that background process in your chest, or in the pit of your stomach. It can make you feel anxious, like when you've had too much coffee or diet coke. It's distracting.

When I am worried about an argument with my wife, or a customer crisis, or a sick child, I can't maintain focus. My concentration wavers. I find myself with my eyes on the screen and my fingers on the keyboard, doing nothing. Catatonic.

Paralyzed. A million miles away working through the problem in the background rather than actually solving the coding problem in front of me.

Sometimes I will force myself to *think* about the code. I might drive myself to write a line or two. I might push myself to get a test or two to pass. But I can't keep it up. Inevitably I find myself descending into a stupefied insensibility, seeing nothing through my open eyes, inwardly churning on the background worry.

I have learned that this is no time to code. Any code I produce will be trash. So instead of coding, I need to resolve the worry.

Of course, there are many worries that simply cannot be resolved in an hour or two. Moreover, our employers are not likely to long tolerate our inability to work as we resolve our personal issues. The trick is to learn how to shut down the background process, or at least reduce its priority so that it's not a continuous distraction.

I do this by partitioning my time. Rather than forcing myself to code while the background worry is nagging at me, I will spend a dedicated block of time, perhaps an hour, working on the issue that is creating the worry. If my child is sick, I will call home and check in. If I've had an argument with my wife, I'll call her and talk through the issues. If I have money problems, I'll spend time thinking about how I can deal with the financial issues. I know I'm not likely to solve the problems in this hour, but it is very likely that I can reduce the anxiety and quiet the background process.

Ideally the time spent wrestling with personal issues would be personal time. It would be a shame to spend an hour at the office this way. Professional developers allocate their personal time in order to ensure that the time spent at the office is as productive as possible. That means you should specifically set aside time at home to settle your anxieties so that you don't bring them to the office.

On the other hand, if you find yourself at the office and the background anxieties are sapping your productivity, then it is better to spend an hour quieting them than to use brute force to write code that you'll just have to throw away later (or worse, live with).

THE FLOW ZONE

Much has been written about the hyper-productive state known as "flow." Some programmers call it "the Zone." Whatever it is called, you are probably familiar with it. It is the highly focused, tunnel-vision state of consciousness that programmers can get into while they write code. In this state they feel *productive*. In this state they feel *infallible*. And so they desire to attain that state, and often measure their self-worth by how much time they can spend there.

Here's a little hint from someone whose been there and back: *Avoid the Zone*. This state of consciousness is not really hyper-productive and is certainly not infallible. It's really just a mild meditative state in which certain rational faculties are diminished in favor of a sense of speed.

Let me be clear about this. You *will* write more code in the Zone. If you are practicing TDD, you will go around the red/green/refactor loop more quickly. And you will *feel* a mild euphoria or a sense of conquest. The problem is that you lose some of the big picture while you are in the Zone, so you will likely make decisions that you will later have to go back and reverse. Code written in the Zone may come out faster, but you'll be going back to visit it more.

Nowadays when I feel myself slipping into the Zone, I walk away for a few minutes. I clear my head by answering a few emails or looking at some tweets. If it's close enough to noon, I'll break for lunch. If I'm working on a team, I'll find a pair partner.

One of the big benefits of pair programming is that it is virtually impossible for a pair to enter the Zone. The Zone is an uncommunicative state, while pairing requires intense and constant communication. Indeed, one of the complaints I often hear about pairing is that it blocks entry into the Zone. Good! The Zone is *not* where you want to be.

Well, that's not *quite* true. There are times when the Zone is exactly where you want to be. When you are *practicing*. But we'll talk about that in another chapter.

MUSIC

At Teradyne, in the late '70s, I had a private office. I was the system administrator of our PDP 11/60, and so I was one of the few programmers allowed to have a private terminal. That terminal was a VT100 running at 9600 baud and connected to the PDP 11 with 80 feet of RS232 cable that I had strung over the ceiling tiles from my office to the computer room.

I had a stereo system in my office. It was an old turntable, amp, and floor speakers. I had a significant collection of vinyl, including Led Zeppelin, Pink Floyd, and …. Well, you get the picture.

I used to crank that stereo and then write code. I thought it helped my concentration. But I was wrong.

One day I went back into a module that I had been editing while listening to the opening sequence of *The Wall*. The comments in that code contained lyrics from the piece, and editorial notations about dive bombers and crying babies.

That's when it hit me. As a reader of the code, I was learning more about the music collection of the author (me) than I was learning about the problem that the code was trying to solve.

I realized that I simply don't code well while listening to music. The music does not help me focus. Indeed, the act of listening to music seems to consume some vital resource that my mind needs in order to write clean and well-designed code.

Maybe it doesn't work that way for you. Maybe music *helps* you write code. I know lots of people who code while wearing earphones. I accept that the music may help them, but I am also suspicious that what's really happening is that the music is helping them enter the Zone.

INTERRUPTIONS

Visualize yourself as you are coding at your workstation. How do you respond when someone asks you a question? Do you snap at them? Do you glare? Does your body-language tell them to go away because you are busy? In short, are you rude?

Or, do you stop what you are doing and politely help someone who is stuck? Do you treat them as you would have them treat you if you were stuck?

The rude response often comes from the Zone. You may resent being dragged out of the Zone, or you may resent someone interfering with your attempt to enter the Zone. Either way, the rudeness often comes from your relationship to the Zone.

Sometimes, however, it's not the Zone that's at fault, it's just that you are trying to understand something complicated that requires concentration. There are several solutions to this.

Pairing can be very helpful as a way to deal with interruptions. Your pair partner can hold the context of the problem at hand, while you deal with a phone call, or a question from a coworker. When you return to your pair partner, he quickly helps you reconstruct the mental context you had before the interruption.

TDD is another big help. If you have a failing test, that test holds the context of where you are. You can return to it after an interruption and continue to make that failing test pass.

In the end, of course, *there will be interruptions* that distract you and cause you to lose time. When they happen, remember that next time you may be the one who needs to interrupt someone else. So the professional attitude is a polite willingness to be helpful.

WRITER'S BLOCK

Sometimes the code just doesn't come. I've had this happen to me and I've seen it happen to others. You sit at your workstation and nothing happens.

Often you will find other work to do. You'll read email. You'll read tweets. You'll look through books, or schedules, or documents. You'll call meetings. You'll start up conversations with others. You'll do *anything* so that you don't have to face that workstation and watch as the code refuses to appear.

What causes such blockages? We've spoken about many of the factors already. For me, another major factor is sleep. If I'm not getting enough sleep, I simply can't code. Others are worry, fear, and depression.

Oddly enough there is a very simple solution. It works almost every time. It's easy to do, and it can provide you with the momentum to get lots of code written.

The solution: Find a pair partner.

It's uncanny how well this works. As soon as you sit down next to someone else, the issues that were blocking you melt away. There is a *physiological* change that takes place when you work with someone. I don't know what it is, but I can definitely feel it. There's some kind of chemical change in my brain or body that breaks me through the blockage and gets me going again.

This is not a perfect solution. Sometimes the change lasts an hour or two, only to be followed by exhaustion so severe that I have to break away from my pair partner and find some hole to recover in. Sometimes, even when sitting with someone, I can't do more than just agree with what that person is doing. But for me the typical reaction to pairing is a recovery of my momentum.

CREATIVE INPUT

There are other things I do to prevent blockage. I learned a long time ago that creative output depends on creative input.

I read a lot, and I read all kinds of material. I read material on software, politics, biology, astronomy, physics, chemistry, mathematics, and much more. However, I find that the thing that best primes the pump of creative output is science fiction.

For you, it might be something else. Perhaps a good mystery novel, or poetry, or even a romance novel. I think the real issue is that creativity breeds creativity. There's also an element of escapism. The hours I spend away from my usual problems, while being actively stimulated by challenging and creative ideas, results in an almost irresistible pressure to create something myself.

Not all forms of creative input work for me. Watching TV does not usually help me create. Going to the movies is better, but only a bit. Listening to music does not help me create code, but does help me create presentations, talks, and videos. Of all the forms of creative input, nothing works better for me than good old space opera.

DEBUGGING

One of the worst debugging sessions in my career happened in 1972. The terminals connected to the Teamsters' accounting system used to freeze once or twice a day. There was no way to force this to happen. The error did not prefer any particular terminals or any particular applications. It didn't matter what the user had been doing before the freeze. One minute the terminal was working fine, and the next minute it was hopelessly frozen.

It took weeks to diagnose this problem. Meanwhile the Teamsters' were getting more and more upset. Every time there was a freeze-up the person at that terminal would have to stop working and wait until they could coordinate all the other users to finish their tasks. Then they'd call us and we'd reboot. It was a nightmare.

We spent the first couple of weeks just gathering data by interviewing the people who experienced the lockups. We'd ask them what they were doing at the time, and what they had done previously. We asked other users if they noticed anything on *their* terminals at the time of the freeze-up. These interviews were all done over the phone because the terminals were located in downtown Chicago, while we worked 30 miles north in the cornfields.

We had no logs, no counters, no debuggers. Our only access to the internals of the system were lights and toggle switches on the front panel. We could stop the computer, and then peek around in memory one word at a time. But we couldn't do this for more than five minutes because the Teamsters' needed their system back up.

We spent a few days writing a simple real-time inspector that could be operated from the ASR-33 teletype that served as our console. With this we could peek and poke around in memory while the system was running. We added log messages that printed on the teletype at critical moments. We created in-memory counters that counted events and remembered state history that we could inspect with the inspector. And, of course, all this had to be written from scratch in assembler and tested in the evenings when the system was not in use.

The terminals were interrupt driven. The characters being sent to the terminals were held in circular buffers. Every time a serial port finished sending a character, an interrupt would fire and the next character in the circular buffer would be readied for sending.

We eventually found that when a terminal froze it was because the three variables that managed the circular buffer were out of sync. We had no idea why this was happening, but at least it was a clue. Somewhere in the 5 KSLOC of supervisory code there was a bug that mishandled one of those pointers.

This new knowledge also allowed us to un-freeze terminals manually! We could poke default values into those three variables using the inspector, and the terminals would magically start running again. Eventually we wrote a little hack that would look through all the counters to see if they were misaligned and repair them. At first we invoked that hack by hitting a special user-interrupt switch on the front panel whenever the Teamsters called to report a freeze-up. Later we simply ran the repair utility once every second.

A month or so later the freeze-up issue was dead, as far as the Teamsters were concerned. Occasionally one of their terminals would pause for a half second or so, but at a base rate of 30 characters per second, nobody seemed to notice.

But why were the counters getting misaligned? I was nineteen and determined to find out.

The supervisory code had been written by Richard, who had since gone off to college. None of the rest of us were familiar with that code because Richard had been quite possessive of it. That code was *his*, and we weren't allowed to know it. But now Richard was gone, so I got out the inches-thick listing and started to go over it page by page.

The circular queues in that system were just FIFO data structures, that is, queues. Application programs pushed characters in one end of the queue until the queue was full. The interrupt heads popped the characters off the other end of the queue when the printer is ready for them. When the queue was empty, the printer would stop. Our bug caused the applications to think that the queue was full, but caused the interrupt heads to think that the queue was empty.

Interrupt heads run in a different "thread" than all other code. So counters and variables that are manipulated by both interrupt heads and other code must be protected from concurrent update. In our case that meant turning the interrupts off around any code that manipulated those three variables. By the time I sat down with that code I knew I was looking for someplace in the code that touched the variables but did not disable the interrupts first.

Nowadays, of course, we'd use the plethora of powerful tools at our disposal to find all the places where the code touched those variables. Within seconds we'd know every line of code that touched them. Within minutes we'd know which did not disable the interrupts. But this was 1972, and I didn't have any tools like that. What I had were my eyes.

I pored over every page of that code, looking for the variables. Unfortunately, the variables were used *everywhere*. Nearly every page touched them in one way or another. Many of those references did not disable the interrupts because they were read-only references and therefore harmless. The problem was, in that particular assembler there was no good way to know if a reference was read-only without following the logic of the code. Any time a variable was read, it might later be updated and stored. And if that happened while the interrupts were enabled, the variables could get corrupted.

It took me days of intense study, but in the end I found it. There, in the middle of the code, was one place where one of the three variables was being updated while the interrupts were enabled.

I did the math. The vulnerability was about two microseconds long. There were a dozen terminals all running at 30 cps, so an interrupt every 3 ms or so. Given the size of the supervisor, and the clock rate of the CPU, we'd expect a freeze-up from this vulnerability one or two times a day. Bingo!

I fixed the problem, of course, but never had the courage to turn off the automatic hack that inspected and fixed the counters. To this day I'm not convinced there wasn't another hole.

DEBUGGING TIME

For some reason software developers don't think of debugging time as coding time. They think of debugging time as a call of nature, something that just *has* to be done. But debugging time is just as expensive to the business as coding time is, and therefore anything we can do to avoid or diminish it is good.

Nowadays I spend much less time debugging than I did ten years ago. I haven't measured the difference, but I believe it's about a factor of ten. I achieved this truly radical reduction in debugging time by adopting the practice of Test Driven Development (TDD), which we'll be discussing in another chapter.

Whether you adopt TDD or some other discipline of equal efficacy,[3] it is incumbent upon you as a professional to reduce your debugging time as close to zero as you can get. Clearly zero is an asymptotic goal, but it is the goal nonetheless.

Doctors don't like to reopen patients to fix something they did wrong. Lawyers don't like to retry cases that they flubbed up. A doctor or lawyer who did that too often would not be considered professional. Likewise, a software developer who creates many bugs is acting unprofessionally.

PACING YOURSELF

Software development is a marathon, not a sprint. You can't win the race by trying to run as fast as you can from the outset. You win by conserving your resources and pacing yourself. A marathon runner takes care of her body both before and *during* the race. Professional programmers conserve their energy and creativity with the same care.

---

3. I don't know of any discipline that is as effective as TDD, but perhaps you do.

KNOW WHEN TO WALK AWAY

Can't go home till you solve this problem? Oh yes you can, and you probably should! Creativity and intelligence are fleeting states of mind. When you are tired, they go away. If you then pound your nonfunctioning brain for hour after late-night hour trying to solve a problem, you'll simply make yourself more tired and reduce the chance that the shower, or the car, will help you solve the problem.

When you are stuck, when you are tired, disengage for awhile. Give your creative subconscious a crack at the problem. You will get more done in less time and with less effort if you are careful to husband your resources. Pace yourself, and your team. Learn your patterns of creativity and brilliance, and take advantage of them rather than work against them.

DRIVING HOME

One place that I have solved a number of problems is my car on the way home from work. Driving requires a lot of noncreative mental resources. You must dedicate your eyes, hands, and portions of your mind to the task; therefore, you must disengage from the problems at work. There is something about *disengagement* that allows your mind to hunt for solutions in a different and more creative way.

THE SHOWER

I have solved an inordinate number of problems in the shower. Perhaps that spray of water early in the morning wakes me up and gets me to review all the solutions that my brain came up with while I was asleep.

When you are working on a problem, you sometimes get so close to it that you can't see all the options. You miss elegant solutions because the creative part of your mind is suppressed by the intensity of your focus. Sometimes the best way to solve a problem is to go home, eat dinner, watch TV, go to bed, and then wake up the next morning and take a shower.

BEING LATE

You *will* be late. It happens to the best of us. It happens to the most dedicated of us. Sometimes we just blow our estimates and wind up late.

The trick to managing lateness is early detection and transparency. The worst case scenario occurs when you continue to tell everyone, up to the very end, that you will be on time—and then let them all down. *Don't* do this. Instead, *regularly* measure your progress against your goal, and come up with three[4] fact-based end dates: best case, nominal case, and worst case. Be as honest as you can about all three dates. *Do not incorporate hope into your estimates!* Present all three numbers to your team and stakeholders. Update these numbers daily.

HOPE

What if these numbers show that you *might* miss a deadline? For example, let's say that there's a trade show in ten days, and we need to have our product there. But let's also say that your three-number estimate for the feature you are working on is 8/12/20.

Do not hope that you can get it all done in ten days! Hope is the project killer. Hope destroys schedules and ruins reputations. Hope will get you into deep trouble. If the trade show is in ten days, and your nominal estimate is 12, you *are not* going to make it. Make sure that the team and the stakeholders understand the situation, and don't let up until there is a fall-back plan. Don't let anyone else have hope.

RUSHING

What if your manager sits you down and asks you to try to make the deadline? What if your manager insists that you "do what it takes"? *Hold to your estimates!* Your original estimates are more accurate than any changes you make while

---

4. There's much more about this in the Estimation chapter.

your boss is confronting you. Tell your boss that you've already considered the options (because you have) and that the only way to improve the schedule is to reduce scope. *Do not be tempted to rush.*

Woe to the poor developer who buckles under pressure and agrees to *try* to make the deadline. That developer will start taking shortcuts and working extra hours in the vain hope of working a miracle. This is a recipe for disaster because it gives you, your team, and your stakeholders false hope. It allows everyone to avoid facing the issue and delays the necessary tough decisions.

There is no way to rush. You can't make yourself code faster. You can't make yourself solve problems faster. If you try, you'll just slow yourself down and make a mess that slows everyone else down, too.

So you must answer your boss, your team, and your stakeholders by depriving them of hope.

OVERTIME

So your boss says, "What if you work an extra two hours a day? What if you work on Saturday? Come on, there's just got to be a way to squeeze enough hours in to get the feature done on time."

Overtime can work, and sometimes it is necessary. Sometimes you can make an otherwise impossible date by putting in some ten-hour days, and a Saturday or two. But this is very risky. You are not likely to get 20% more work done by working 20% more hours. What's more, overtime will *certainly* fail if it goes on for more than two or three weeks.

Therefore you should *not* agree to work overtime unless (1) you can personally afford it, (2) it is short term, two weeks or less, and (3) *your boss has a fall-back plan* in case the overtime effort fails.

That last criterion is a deal breaker. If your boss cannot articulate to you what he's going to do if the overtime effort fails, then you should not agree to work overtime.

FALSE DELIVERY

Of all the unprofessional behaviors that a programmer can indulge in, perhaps the worst of all is saying you are done when you know you aren't. Sometimes this is just an overt lie, and that's bad enough. But the far more insidious case is when we manage to rationalize a new definition of "done." We convince ourselves that we are done *enough*, and move on to the next task. We rationalize that any work that remains can be dealt with later when we have more time.

This is a contagious practice. If one programmer does it, others will see and follow suit. One of them will stretch the definition of "done" even more, and everyone else will adopt the new definition. I've seen this taken to horrible extremes. One of my clients actually defined "done" as "checked-in." The code didn't even have to compile. It's very easy to be "done" if nothing has to work!

When a team falls into this trap, managers hear that everything is going fine. All status reports show that everyone is on time. It's like blind men having a picnic on the railroad tracks: Nobody sees the freight train of unfinished work bearing down on them until it is too late.

DEFINE "DONE"

You avoid the problem of false delivery by creating an independent definition of "done." The best way to do this is to have your business analysts and testers create automated acceptance tests[5] that must pass before you can say that you are done. These tests should be written in a testing language such as FITNESSE, Selenium, RobotFX, Cucumber, and so on. The tests should be understandable by the stakeholders and business people, and should be run frequently.

HELP

Programming is *hard*. The younger you are the less you believe this. After all, it's just a bunch of if and while statements. But as you gain experience you begin to realize that the way you combine those if and while statements is critically

---

5. See Chapter 7, "Acceptance Testing."

important. You can't just slather them together and hope for the best. Rather, you have to carefully partition the system into small understandable units that have as little to do with each other as possible—and that's hard.

Programming is so hard, in fact, that it is beyond the capability of one person do it well. No matter how skilled you are, you will certainly benefit from another programmer's thoughts and ideas.

HELPING OTHERS

Because of this, it is the responsibility of programmers to be available to help each other. It is a violation of professional ethics to sequester yourself in a cubicle or office and refuse the queries of others. Your work is not so important that you cannot lend some of your time to help others. Indeed, as a professional you are honor bound to offer that help whenever it is needed.

This doesn't mean that you don't need some alone time. Of course you do. But you have to be fair and polite about it. For example, you can let it be known that between the hours of 10 AM and noon you should not be bothered, but from 1 PM to 3 PM your door is open.

You should be conscious of the status of your teammates. If you see someone who appears to be in trouble, you should offer your help. You will likely be quite surprised at the profound effect your help can have. It's not that you are so much smarter than the other person, it's just that a fresh perspective can be a profound catalyst for solving problems.

When you help someone, sit down and write code together. Plan to spend the better part of an hour or more. It may take less than that, but you don't want to appear to be rushed. Resign yourself to the task and give it a solid effort. You will likely come away having learned more than you gave.

BEING HELPED

When someone offers to help you, be gracious about it. Accept the help gratefully and give yourself to that help. *Do not protect your turf.* Do not push the help away because you are under the gun. Give it thirty minutes or so. If by that time the person is not really helping all that much, then politely excuse yourself and terminate the session with thanks. Remember, just as you are honor bound to offer help, you are honor bound to accept help.

Learn how to *ask* for help. When you are stuck, or befuddled, or just can't wrap your mind around a problem, ask someone for help. If you are sitting in a team room, you can just sit back and say, "I need some help." Otherwise, use yammer, or twitter, or email, or the phone on your desk. Call for help. Again, this is a matter of professional ethics. It is unprofessional to remain stuck when help is easily accessible.

By this time you may be expecting me to burst into a chorus of *Kumbaya* while fuzzy bunnies leap onto the backs of unicorns and we all happily fly over rainbows of hope and change. No, not quite. You see, programmers *tend* to be arrogant, self-absorbed introverts. We didn't get into this business because we like *people.* Most of us got into programming because we prefer to deeply focus on sterile minutia, juggle lots of concepts simultaneously, and in general prove to ourselves that we have brains the size of a planet, all while not having to interact with the messy complexities of *other people.*

Yes, this is a stereotype. Yes, it is generalization with many exceptions. But the reality is that programmers do not tend to be collaborators.[6] And yet collaboration is critical to effective programming. Therefore, since for many of us collaboration is not an instinct, we require *disciplines* that drive us to collaborate.

MENTORING

I have a whole chapter on this topic later in the book. For now let me simply say that the training of less experienced programmers is the responsibility of those who have more experience. Training courses don't cut it. Books don't cut it. Nothing can bring a young software developer to high performance quicker

---

6. This is far more true of men than women. I had a wonderful conversation with @desi (Desi McAdam, founder of DevChix) about what motivates women programmers. I told her that when I got a program working, it was like slaying the great beast. She told me that for her and other women she had spoken to, the act of writing code was an act of nurturing creation.

than his own drive, and effective mentoring by his seniors. Therefore, once again, it is a matter of professional ethics for senior programmers to spend time taking younger programmers under their wing and mentoring them. By the same token, those younger programmers have a professional duty to seek out such mentoring from their seniors.

BIBLIOGRAPHY

[**Martin09**]: Robert C. Martin, *Clean Code*, Upper Saddle River, NJ: Prentice Hall, 2009.

[**Martin03**]: Robert C. Martin, *Agile Software Development: Principles, Patterns, and Practices*, Upper Saddle River, NJ: Prentice Hall, 2003.

TEST 5 DRIVEN DEVELOPMENT

It has been over ten years since Test Driven Development (TDD) made its debut in the industry. It came in as part of the Extreme Programming (XP) wave, but has since been adopted by Scrum, and virtually all of the other Agile methods. Even non-Agile teams practice TDD.

When, in 1998, I first heard of "Test First Programming" I was skeptical. Who wouldn't be? Write your unit tests *first*? Who would do a goofy thing like that?

But I'd been a professional programmer for thirty years by then, and I'd seen things come and go in the industry. I knew better than to dismiss anything out of hand, especially when someone like Kent Beck says it.

So in 1999 I travelled to Medford, Oregon, to meet with Kent and learn the discipline from him. The whole experience was a shocker!

Kent and I sat down in his office and started to code some simple little problem in Java. I wanted to just write the silly thing. But Kent resisted and took me, step by step, through the process. First he wrote a small part of a unit test, barely enough to qualify as code. Then he wrote just enough code to make that test compile. Then he wrote a little more test, then more code.

The cycle time was completely outside my experience. I was used to writing code for the better part of an hour before trying to compile or run it. But Kent was literally executing his code every thirty seconds or so. I was flabbergasted!

What's more, I recognized the cycle time! It was the kind of cycle time I'd used years before as a kid[1] programming games in interpreted languages like Basic or Logo. In those languages there is no build time, so you just add a line of code and then execute. You go around the cycle very quickly. And because of that, you can be *very* productive in those languages.

But in *real* programming that kind of cycle time was absurd. In *real* programming you had to spend lots of time writing code, and then lots more time getting it to compile. And then even more time debugging it. *I was a C++ programmer, dammit!* And in C++ we had build and link times that took minutes, sometimes hours. Thirty-second cycle times were unimaginable.

Yet there was Kent, cooking away at this Java program in thirty-second cycles and without any hint that he'd be slowing down any time soon. So it dawned on me, while I sat there in Kent's office, that using this simple discipline I could code in real languages with the cycle time of Logo! I was hooked!

---

1. From my vantage point at the time a kid is anyone younger than 35. During my twenties I spent a significant amount of time writing silly little games in interpreted languages. I wrote space war games, adventure games, horse race games, snake games, gambling games, you name it.

THE JURY IS IN

Since those days I've learned that TDD is much more than a simple trick to shorten my cycle time. The discipline has a whole repertoire of benefits that I'll describe in the following paragraphs.

But first I need to say this:

- The jury is in!
- The controversy is over.
- GOTO is harmful.
- And TDD works.

Yes, there have been lots of controversial blogs and articles written about TDD over the years and there still are. In the early days they were serious attempts at critique and understanding. Nowadays, however, they are just rants. The bottom line is that TDD works, and everybody needs to get over it.

I know this sounds strident and unilateral, but given the record I don't think surgeons should have to defend hand-washing, and I don't think programmers should have to defend TDD.

How can you consider yourself to be a professional if you do not *know* that all your code works? How can you know all your code works if you don't test it every time you make a change? How can you test it every time you make a change if you don't have automated unit tests with very high coverage? How can you get automated unit tests with very high coverage without practicing TDD?

That last sentence requires some elaboration. Just what is TDD?

THE THREE LAWS OF TDD

1. You are not allowed to write any production code until you have first written a failing unit test.
2. You are not allowed to write more of a unit test than is sufficient to fail—and not compiling is failing.

3. You are not allowed to write more production code that is sufficient to pass the currently failing unit test.

These three laws lock you into a cycle that is, perhaps, thirty seconds long. You begin by writing a small portion of a unit test. But within a few seconds you must mention the name of some class or function you have not written yet, thereby causing the unit test to fail to compile. So you must write production code that makes the test compile. But you can't write any more than that, so you start writing more unit test code.

Round and round the cycle you go. Adding a bit to the test code. Adding a bit to the production code. The two code streams grow simultaneously into complementary components. The tests fit the production code like an antibody fits an antigen.

THE LITANY OF BENEFITS

Certainty

If you adopt TDD as a professional discipline, then you will write dozens of tests every day, hundreds of tests every week, and thousands of tests every year. And you will keep all those tests on hand and run them any time you make any changes to the code.

I am the primary author and maintainer of FITNESSE,[2] a Java-based acceptance testing tool. As of this writing FITNESSE is 64,000 lines of code, of which 28,000 are contained in just over 2,200 individual unit tests. These tests cover at least 90% of the production code[3] and take about 90 seconds to run.

Whenever I make a change to any part of FITNESSE, I simply run the unit tests. If they pass, I am nearly certain that the change I made didn't break anything. How certain is "nearly certain"? Certain enough to ship!

The QA process for FITNESSE is the command: ant release. That command builds FITNESSE from scratch and then runs all the unit and acceptance tests. If those tests all pass, I ship it.

---

2. http://fitnesse.org
3. Ninety percent is a minimum. The number is actually larger than that. The exact amount is hard to calculate because the coverage tools can't see code that runs in external processes or in catch blocks.

Defect Injection Rate

Now, FITNESSE is not a mission-critical application. If there's a bug, nobody dies, and nobody loses millions of dollars. So I can afford to ship based on nothing but passing tests. On the other hand, FITNESSE has thousands of users, and despite the addition of 20,000 new lines of code last year, my bug list only has 17 bugs on it (many of which are cosmetic in nature). So I know my defect injection rate is very low.

This is not an isolated effect. There have been several reports[4] and studies[5] that describe significant defect reduction. From IBM, to Microsoft, from Sabre to Symantec, company after company and team after team have experienced defect reductions of 2X, 5X, and even 10X. These are numbers that no professional should ignore.

Courage

Why don't you fix bad code when you see it? Your first reaction upon seeing a messy function is "This is a mess, it needs to be cleaned." Your second reaction is "I'm not touching it!" Why? Because you know that if you touch it you risk breaking it; and if you break it, it becomes yours.

But what if you could be *sure* that your cleaning did not break anything? What if you had the kind of certainty that I just mentioned? What if you could click a button and *know* within 90 seconds that your changes had broken nothing, *and had only done good?*

This is one of the most powerful benefits of TDD. When you have a suite of tests that you trust, then you lose all fear of making changes. When you see bad code, you simply clean it on the spot. The code becomes clay that you can safely sculpt into simple and pleasing structures.

When programmers lose the fear of cleaning, they clean! And clean code is easier to understand, easier to change, and easier to extend. Defects become

---

4. http://www.objectmentor.com/omSolutions/agile_customers.html
5. [Maximilien], [George2003], [Janzen2005], [Nagappan2008]

even less likely because the code gets simpler. And the code base steadily *improves* instead of the normal rotting that our industry has become used to.

What professional programmer would allow the rotting to continue?

Documentation

Have you ever used a third-party framework? Often the third party will send you a nicely formatted manual written by tech writers. The typical manual employs 27 eight-by-ten color glossy photographs with circles and arrows and a paragraph on the back of each one explaining how to configure, deploy, manipulate, and otherwise use that framework. At the back, in the appendix, there's often an ugly little section that contains all the code examples.

Where's the first place you go in that manual? If you are a programmer, you go to the code examples. You go to the code because you know the code will tell you the truth. The 27 eight-by-ten color glossy photographs with circles and arrows and a paragraph on the back might be pretty, but if you want to know how to use code you need to read code.

Each of the unit tests you write when you follow the three laws is an example, written in code, describing how the system should be used. If you follow the three laws, then there will be a unit test that describes how to create every object in the system, every way that those objects can be created. There will be a unit test that describes how to call every function in the system every way that those functions can meaningfully be called. For anything you need to know how to do, there will be a unit test that describes it in detail.

The unit tests are documents. They describe the lowest-level design of the system. They are unambiguous, accurate, written in a language that the audience understands, and are so formal that they execute. They are the best kind of low-level documentation that can exist. What professional would not provide such documentation?

Design

When you follow the three laws and write your tests first, you are faced with a dilemma. Often you know exactly what code you want to write, but the three laws tell you to write a unit test that fails because that code doesn't exist! This means you have to test the code that you are about to write.

The problem with testing code is that you have to isolate that code. It is often difficult to test a function if that function calls other functions. To write that test you've got to figure out some way to decouple the function from all the others. In other words, the need to test first forces you to think about *good design*.

If you don't write your tests first, there is no force preventing you from coupling the functions together into an untestable mass. If you write your tests later, you may be able to test the inputs and the outputs of the total mass, but it will probably be quite difficult to test the individual functions.

Therefore, following the three laws, and writing your tests first, creates a force that drives you to a better decoupled design. What professional would not employ tools that drove them toward better designs?

"But I can write my tests later," you say. No, you can't. Not really. Oh, you can write *some* tests later. You can even approach high coverage later if you are careful to measure it. But the tests you write after the fact are *defense*. The tests you write first are *offense*. After-the-fact tests are written by someone who is already vested in the code and already knows how the problem was solved. There's just no way those tests can be anywhere near as incisive as tests written first.

THE PROFESSIONAL OPTION

The upshot of all this is that TDD is the professional option. It is a discipline that enhances certainty, courage, defect reduction, documentation, and design. With all that going for it, it could be considered *unprofessional* not to use it.

WHAT TDD IS NOT

For all its good points, TDD is not a religion or a magic formula. Following the three laws does not guarantee any of these benefits. You can still write bad code even if you write your tests first. Indeed, you can write bad tests.

By the same token, there are times when following the three laws is simply impractical or inappropriate. These situations are rare, but they exist. No professional developer should ever follow a discipline when that discipline does more harm than good.

BIBLIOGRAPHY

[**Maximilien**]: E. Michael Maximilien, Laurie Williams, "Assessing Test-Driven Development at IBM," http://collaboration.csc.ncsu.edu/laurie/Papers/MAXIMILIEN_WILLIAMS.PDF

[**George2003**]: B. George, and L. Williams, "An Initial Investigation of Test-Driven Development in Industry," http://collaboration.csc.ncsu.edu/laurie/Papers/TDDpaperv8.pdf

[**Janzen2005**]: D. Janzen and H. Saiedian, "Test-driven development concepts, taxonomy, and future direction," *IEEE Computer*, Volume 38, Issue 9, pp. 43–50.

[**Nagappan2008**]: Nachiappan Nagappan, E. Michael Maximilien, Thirumalesh Bhat, and Laurie Williams, "Realizing quality improvement through test driven development: results and experiences of four industrial teams," Springer Science + Business Media, LLC 2008: http://research.microsoft.com/en-us/projects/esm/nagappan_tdd.pdf

6 PRACTICING

All professionals practice their art by engaging in skill-sharpening exercises. Musicians rehearse scales. Football players run through tires. Doctors practice sutures and surgical techniques. Lawyers practice arguments. Soldiers rehearse missions. When performance matters, professionals practice. This chapter is all about the ways in which programmers can practice their art.

SOME BACKGROUND ON PRACTICING

Practicing is not a new concept in software development, but we didn't recognize it as practicing until just after the turn of the millennium. Perhaps the first formal instance of a practice program was printed on page 6 of [K&R-C].

```
main()
{
    printf("hello, world\n");
}
```

Who among us has not written that program in one form or another? We use it as a way to prove a new environment or a new language. Writing and executing that program is proof that we can write and execute *any* program.

When I was much younger, one of the first programs I would write on a new computer was SQINT, the squares of integers. I wrote it in assembler, BASIC, FORTRAN, COBOL, and a zillion other languages. Again, it was a way to prove that I could make the computer do what I wanted it to do.

In the early '80s personal computers first started to show up in department stores. Whenever I passed one, like a VIC-20 or a Commodore-64, or a TRS-80, I would write a little program that printed an infinite stream of '\' and '/' characters on the screen. The patterns this program produced were pleasing to the eye and looked far more complex than the little program that generated them.

Although these little programs were certainly practice programs, programmers in general did not *practice*. Frankly, the thought never occurred to us. We were too busy writing code to think about practicing our skills. And besides, what would have been the point? During those years programming did not require quick reactions or nimble fingers. We did not use screen editors until the late '70s. We spent much of our time waiting for compiles or debugging long, horrid stretches of code. We had not yet invented the short-cycles of TDD, so we did not require the fine-tuning that practice could bring.

TWENTY-TWO ZEROS

But things have changed since the early days of programming. Some things have changed a *lot*. Other things haven't changed much at all.

One of the first machines I ever wrote programs for was a PDP-8/I. This machine had a 1.5-microsecond cycle time. It had 4,096 12-bit words in core memory. It was the size of a refrigerator and consumed a significant amount of electrical power. It had a disk drive that could store 32K of 12-bit words, and we talked to it with a 10-character-per-second teletype. We thought this was a *powerful* machine, and we used it to work miracles.

I just bought a new Macbook Pro laptop. It has a 2.8GHz dual core processor, 8GB of RAM, a 512GB SSD, and a 17-inch 1920 × 1200 LED screen. I carry it in my backpack. It sits on my lap. It consumes less than 85 watts.

My laptop is eight thousand times faster, has two million times more memory, has sixteen million times more offline storage, requires 1% of the power, takes up 1% of the space, and costs one twenty-fifth of the price of the PDP-8/I. Let's do the math:

$$8,000 \times 2,000,000 \times 16,000,000 \times 100 \times 100 \times 25 = 6.4 \times 10^{22}$$

This number is *large*. We're talking about *22 orders of magnitude!* That's how many angstroms there are between here and Alpha Centauri. That's how many electrons there are in a silver dollar. That's the mass of the Earth in units of Michael Moore. This is a big, big, number. And it's sitting in my lap, and probably yours too!

And what am I doing with this increase in power of 22 factors of ten? I'm doing pretty much what I was doing with that PDP-8/I. I'm writing *if* statements, *while* loops, and *assignments*.

Oh, I've got better tools to write those statements with. And I have better languages to write those statements with. But the nature of the statements hasn't changed in all that time. Code in 2010 would be recognizable to a programmer from the 1960s. The clay that we manipulate has not changed much in those four decades.

TURNAROUND TIME

But the *way* we work has changed dramatically. In the '60s I could wait a day or two to see the results of a compile. In the late '70s a 50,000-line program might take 45 minutes to compile. Even in the '90s, long build times were the norm.

Programmers today don't wait for compiles.[1] Programmers today have such immense power under their fingers that they can spin around the red-green-refactor loop in seconds.

For example, I work on a 64,000-line Java project named FITNESSE. A full build, including *all* unit and integration tests, executes in less than 4 minutes. If those tests pass, I'm ready to ship the product. *So the whole QA process, from source code to deployment, requires less than 4 minutes.* Compiles take almost no measurable time at all. Partial tests require *seconds.* So I can literally spin around the compile/test loop *ten times per minute*!

It's not always wise to go that fast. Often it is better to slow down and just *think*.[2] But there are other times when spinning around that loop as fast as possible is *highly* productive.

Doing anything quickly requires practice. Spinning around the code/test loop quickly requires you to make very quick decisions. Making decisions quickly means being able to recognize a vast number of situations and problems and simply *know* what to do to address them.

Consider two martial artists in combat. Each must recognize what the other is attempting and respond appropriately within milliseconds. In a combat situation you don't have the luxury of freezing time, studying the positions, and deliberating on the appropriate response. In a combat situation you simply have to *react*. Indeed, it is your *body* that reacts while your mind is working on a higher-level strategy.

---

1. The fact that some programmers do wait for builds is tragic and indicative of carelessness. In today's world build times should be measured in seconds, not minutes, and certainly not hours.
2. This is a technique that Rich Hickey calls HDD, or Hammock-Driven Development.

When you are spinning around the code/test loop several times per minute, it is your *body* that knows what keys to hit. A primal part of your mind recognizes the situation and reacts within milliseconds with the appropriate solution while your mind is free to focus on the higher-level problem.

In both the martial arts case and the programming case, speed depends on *practice*. And in both cases the practice is similar. We choose a repertoire of problem/solution pairs and execute them over and over again until we know them cold.

Consider a guitarist like Carlos Santana. The music in his head simply comes out his fingers. He does not focus on finger positions or picking technique. His mind is free to plan out higher-level melodies and harmonies while his body translates those plans into lower-level finger motions.

But to gain that kind of ease of play requires *practice*. Musicians practice scales and études and riffs over and over until they know them cold.

THE CODING DOJO

Since 2001 I have been performing a TDD demonstration that I call *The Bowling Game*.[3] It's a lovely little exercise that takes about thirty minutes. It experiences conflict in the design, builds to a climax, and ends with a surprise. I wrote a whole chapter on this example in [PPP2003].

Over the years I performed this demonstration hundreds, perhaps thousands, of times. I got *very* good at it! I could do it in my sleep. I minimized the keystrokes, tuned the variable names, and tweaked the algorithm structure until it was just right. Although I didn't know it at the time, this was my first kata.

In 2005 I attended the XP2005 Conference in Sheffield, England. I attended a session with the name *Coding Dojo* led by Laurent Bossavit and Emmanuel Gaillot. They had everyone open their laptops and code along with them as they

---

3. This has become a very popular kata, and a Google search will find many instances of it. The original is here: http://butunclebob.com/ArticleS.UncleBob.TheBowlingGameKata.

used TDD to write Conway's *Game of Life.* They called it a "Kata" and credited "Pragmatic" Dave Thomas[4] with the original idea.[5]

Since then many programmers have adopted a martial arts metaphor for their practice sessions. The name Coding Dojo[6] seems to have stuck. Sometimes a group of programmers will meet and practice together just like martial artists do. At other times, programmers will practice solo, again as martial artists do.

About a year ago I was teaching a group of developers in Omaha. At lunch they invited me to join their Coding Dojo. I watched as twenty developers opened their laptops and, keystroke by keystroke, followed along with the leader who was doing *The Bowling Game* Kata.

There are several kinds of activities that take place in a dojo. Here are a few:

KATA

In martial arts, a *kata* is a precise set of choreographed movements that simulates one side of a combat. The goal, which is asymptotically approached, is perfection. The artist strives to teach his body to make each movement perfectly and to assemble those movements into fluid enactment. Well-executed kata are beautiful to watch.

Beautiful though they are, the purpose of learning a kata is not to perform it on stage. The purpose is to train your mind and body how to react in a particular combat situation. The goal is to make the perfected movements automatic and instinctive so that they are there when you need them.

A programming kata is a precise set of choreographed keystrokes and mouse movements that simulates the solving of some programming problem. You aren't actually solving the problem because you already know the solution. Rather, you are practicing the movements and decisions involved in solving the problem.

---

4. We use the "Pragmatic" prefix to disambiguate him from "Big" Dave Thomas from OTI.
5. http://codekata.pragprog.com
6. http://codingdojo.org/

The asymptote of perfection is once again the goal. You repeat the exercise over and over again to train your brain and fingers how to move and react. As you practice you may discover subtle improvements and efficiencies either in your motions or in the solution itself.

Practicing a suite of katas is a good way to learn hot keys and navigation idioms. It is also a good way to learn disciplines such as TDD and CI. But most importantly, it is a good way to drive common problem/solution pairs into your subconscious, so that you simply know how to solve them when facing them in real programming.

Like any martial artist, a programmer should know several different kata and practice them regularly so that they don't fade away from memory. Many kata are recorded at http://katas.softwarecraftsmanship.org. Others can be found at http://codekata.pragprog.com. Some of my favorites are:

- *The Bowling Game:* http://butunclebob.com/ArticleS.UncleBob.TheBowling-GameKata
- *Prime Factors:* http://butunclebob.com/ArticleS.UncleBob.ThePrimeFactors-Kata
- *Word Wrap:* http://thecleancoder.blogspot.com/2010/10/craftsman-62-dark-path.html

For a real challenge, try learning a kata so well that you can set it to music. Doing this well is *hard.*[7]

Wasa

When I studied jujitsu, much of our time in the dojo was spent in pairs practicing our *wasa*. Wasa is very much like a two-man kata. The routines are precisely memorized and played back. One partner plays the role of the aggressor, and the other partner is the defender. The motions are repeated over and over again as the practitioners swap roles.

---

7. http://katas.softwarecraftsmanship.org/?p=71

Programmers can practice in a similar fashion using a game known as *ping-pong*.[8] The two partners choose a kata, or a simple problem. One programmer writes a unit test, and then the other must make it pass. Then they reverse roles.

If the partners choose a standard kata, then the outcome is known and the programmers are practicing and critiquing each other's keyboarding and mousing techniques, and how well they've memorized the kata. On the other hand, if the partners choose a new problem to solve, then the game can get a bit more interesting. The programmer writing a test has an inordinate amount of control over how the problem will be solved. He also has a significant amount of power to set constraints. For example, if the programmers choose to implement a sort algorithm, the test writer can easily put constraints on speed and memory space that will challenge his partner. This can make the game quite competative . . . and fun.

RANDORI

Randori is free-form combat. In our jujitsu dojo, we would set up a variety of combat scenarios and then enact them. Sometimes one person was told to defend, while each of the rest of us would attack him in sequence. Sometimes we would set two or more attackers against a single defender (usually the sensei, who almost always won). Sometimes we'd do two on two, and so forth.

Simulated combat does not map well to programming; however, there is a game that is played at many coding dojos called randori. It is very much like two-man wasa in which the partners are solving a problem. However, it is played with many people and the rules have a twist. With the screen projected on the wall, one person writes a test and then sits down. The next person makes the test pass and then writes the next test. This can be done in sequence around the table, or people can simply line up as they feel so moved. In either case these exercises can be a *lot* of fun.

---

8. http://c2.com/cgi/wiki?PairProgrammingPingPongPattern

It is remarkable how much you can learn from these sessions. You can gain an immense insight into the way other people solve problems. These insights can only serve to broaden your own approach and improve your skill.

BROADENING YOUR EXPERIENCE

Professional programmers often suffer from a lack of diversity in the kinds of problems that they solve. Employers often enforce a single language, platform, and domain in which their programmers must work. Without a broadening influence, this can lead to a very unhealthy narrowing of your resume and your mindset. It is not uncommon for such programmers to find themselves unprepared for the changes that periodically sweep the industry.

OPEN SOURCE

One way to stay ahead of the curve is to do what lawyers and doctors do: Take on some pro-bono work by contributing to an open-source project. There are lots of them out there, and there is probably no better way to increase your repertoire of skills than to actually work on something that someone else cares about.

So if you are a Java programmer, contribute to a Rails project. If you write a lot of C++ for your employer, find a Python project and contribute to it.

PRACTICE ETHICS

Professional programmers practice on their own time. It is not your employer's job to help you keep your skills sharp for you. It is not your employer's job to help you keep your resume tuned. Patients do not pay doctors to practice sutures. Football fans do not (usually) pay to see players run through tires. Concert-goers do not pay to hear musicians play scales. And employers of programmers don't have to pay you for your practice time.

Since your practice time is your own time, you don't have to use the same languages or platforms that you use with your employer. Pick any language you like and keep your polyglot skills sharp. If you work in a .NET shop, practice a little Java or Ruby at lunch, or at home.

CONCLUSION

In one way or another, *all* professionals practice. They do this because they care about doing the best job they possibly can. What's more, they practice on their own time because they realize that it is their responsibility—and not their employer's—to keep their skills sharp. Practicing is what you do when you *aren't* getting paid. You do it so that you *will* be paid, and paid *well*.

BIBLIOGRAPHY

[**K&R-C**]: Brian W. Kernighan and Dennis M. Ritchie, *The C Programming Language,* Upper Saddle River, NJ: Prentice Hall, 1975.

[**PPP2003**]: Robert C. Martin, *Agile Software Development: Principles, Patterns, and Practices,* Upper Saddle River, NJ: Prentice Hall, 2003.

ACCEPTANCE TESTING

7

The role of the professional developer is a communications role as well as a development role. Remember that garbage-in/garbage-out applies to programmers too, so professional programmers are careful to make sure that their communication with other members of the team, and the business, are accurate and healthy.

COMMUNICATING REQUIREMENTS

One of the most common communication issues between programmers and business is the requirements. The business people state what they believe they need, and then the programmers build what they believe the business described. At least that's how it's supposed to work. In reality, the communication of requirements is extremely difficult, and the process is fraught with error.

In 1979, while working at Teradyne, I had a visit from Tom, the manager of installation and field service. He asked me to show him how to use the ED-402 text editor to create a simple trouble-ticket system.

ED-402 was a proprietary editor written for the M365 computer, which was Teradyne's PDP-8 clone. As a text editor it was very powerful. It had a built-in scripting language that we used for all kinds of simple text applications.

Tom was not a programmer. But the application he had in mind was simple, so he thought I could teach him quickly and then he could write the application himself. In my naivete I thought the same thing. After all, the scripting language was little more than a macro language for the editing commands, with very rudimentary decision and looping constructs.

So we sat down together and I asked him what he wanted his application to do. He started with the initial entry screen. I showed him how to create a text file that would hold the script statements and how to type the symbolic representation of the edit commands into that script. But when I looked into his eyes, there was nothing looking back. My explanation simply made no sense to him at all.

This was the first time I had encountered this. For me it was a simple thing to represent editor commands symbolically. For example, to represent a control-B command (the command that puts the cursor at the beginning of the current line) you simply typed ^B into the script file. But this made no sense to Tom. He couldn't make the leap from editing a file to editing a file that edited a file.

Tom wasn't dumb. I think he simply realized that this was going to be a lot more involved than he initially thought, and he didn't want to invest the time and mental energy necessary to learn something so hideously convoluted as using an editor to command an editor.

So bit by bit I found myself implementing this application while he sat there and watched. Within the first twenty minutes it was clear that his emphasis had changed from learning how to do it himself to making sure that what *I* did was what *he* wanted.

It took us an entire day. He would describe a feature and I would implement it as he watched. The cycle time was five minutes or less, so there was no reason for him to get up and do anything else. He'd ask me to do X, and within five minutes I had X working.

Often he would draw what he wanted on a scrap of paper. Some of the things he wanted were hard to do in ED-402, so I'd propose something else. We'd eventually agree on something that would work, and then I'd make it work.

But then we'd try it and he'd change his mind. He'd say something like, "Yeah, that just doesn't have the flow I'm looking for. Let's try it a different way."

Hour after hour we fiddled and poked and prodded that application into shape. We tried one thing, then another, and then another. It became very clear to me that *he* was the sculptor, and I was the tool he was wielding.

In the end, he got the application he was looking for but had no idea how to go about building the next one for himself. I, on the other hand, learned a powerful lesson about how customers actually discover what they need. I learned that their vision of the features does not often survive actual contact with the computer.

PREMATURE PRECISION

Both business and programmers are tempted to fall into the trap of premature precision. Business people want to know exactly what they are going to get before they authorize a project. Developers want to know exactly what they are supposed to deliver before they estimate the project. Both sides want a precision that simply cannot be achieved, and are often willing to waste a fortune trying to attain it.

The Uncertainty Principle

The problem is that things appear different on paper than they do in a working system. When the business actually sees what they specified running in a system, they realize that it wasn't what they wanted at all. Once they see the requirement actually running, they have a better idea of what they really want—and it's usually not what they are seeing.

There's a kind of observer effect, or uncertainty principle, in play. When you demonstrate a feature to the business, it gives them more information than they had before, and that new information impacts how they see the whole system.

In the end, the more precise you make your requirements, the less relevant they become as the system is implemented.

Estimation Anxiety

Developers, too, can get caught in the precision trap. They know they must estimate the system and often think that this requires precision. It doesn't.

First, even with perfect information your estimates will have a huge variance. Second, the uncertainty principle makes hash out of early precision. The requirements *will* change making that precision moot.

Professional developers understand that estimates can, and should, be made based on low precision requirements, and recognize that those estimates *are estimates*. To reinforce this, professional developers always include error bars with their estimates so that the business understands the uncertainty. (See Chapter 10, "Estimation.")

LATE AMBIGUITY

The solution to premature precision is to defer precision as long as possible. Professional developers don't flesh out a requirement until they are just about to develop it. However, that can lead to another malady: late ambiguity.

Often stakeholders disagree. When they do, they may find it easier to *wordsmith* their way around the disagreement rather than solve it. They will find some way of phrasing the requirement that they can all agree with, without actually resolving the dispute. I once heard Tom DeMarco say, "An ambiguity in a requirements document represents an argument amongst the stakeholders."[1]

Of course, it doesn't take an argument or a disagreement to create ambiguity. Sometimes the stakeholders simply assume that their readers know what they mean.

---

1. XP Immersion 3, May, 2000. http://c2.com/cgi/wiki?TomsTalkAtXpImmersionThree

It may be perfectly clear to them in their context, but mean something completely different to the programmer who reads it. This kind of contextual ambiguity can also occur when customers and programmers are speaking face to face.

> Sam (stakeholder): "OK, now these log files need to be backed up."
>
> Paula: "OK, how often?"
>
> Sam: "Daily."
>
> Paula: "Right. And where do you want it saved?"
>
> Sam: "What do you mean?"
>
> Paula: "Do you want me to save it a particular sub-directory?"
>
> Sam: "Yes, that'd be good."
>
> Paula: "What shall we call it?"
>
> Sam: "How about 'backup'?"
>
> Paula: "Sure, that'd be fine. So we'll write the log file into the backup directory every day. What time?"
>
> Sam: "Every day."
>
> Paula: "No, I mean what time of day do you want it written?"
>
> Sam: "Any time."
>
> Paula: "Noon?"
>
> Sam: "No, not during trading hours. Midnight would be better."
>
> Paula: "OK, midnight then."
>
> Sam: "Great, thanks!"
>
> Paula: "Always a pleasure."

Later, Paula is telling her teammate Peter about the task.

> Paula: "OK, we need to copy the log file into a sub-directory named backup every night at midnight."
>
> Peter: "OK, what file name should we use?"
>
> Paula: "log.backup ought to do it."
>
> Peter: "You got it."

In a different office, Sam is on the phone with his customer.

Sam: "Yes, yes, the log files will be saved."

Carl: "OK, it's vital that we never lose any logs. We need to go back through all those log files, even months or years later, whenever there's an outage, event, or dispute."

Sam: "Don't worry, I just spoke to Paula. She'll be saving the logs into a directory named backup every night at midnight."

Carl: "OK, that sounds good."

I presume you've detected the ambiguity. The customer expects all log files to be saved, and Paula simply thought they wanted to save last night's log file. When the customer goes looking for months' worth of log file backups, they'll just find last night's.

In this case both Paula and Sam dropped the ball. It is the responsibility of professional developers (and stakeholders) to make sure that all ambiguity is removed from the requirements.

This is *hard*, and there's only one way I know how to do it.

ACCEPTANCE TESTS

The term *acceptance test* is overloaded and overused. Some folks assume that these are the tests that users execute before they accept a release. Other folks think these are QA tests. In this chapter we will define acceptance tests as tests written by a collaboration of the stakeholders and the programmers *in order to define when a requirement is done*.

THE DEFINITION OF "DONE"

One of the most common ambiguities we face as software professionals is the ambiguity of "done." When a developer says he's done with a task, what does that mean? Is the developer done in the sense that he's ready to deploy the feature with full confidence? Or does he mean that he's ready for QA? Or perhaps he's done writing it and has gotten it to run once but hasn't really tested it yet.

I have worked with teams who had a different definition for the words "done" and "complete." One particular team used the terms "done" and "done-done."

Professional developers have a single definition of done: Done means *done*. Done means all code written, all tests pass, QA and the stakeholders have accepted. Done.

But how can you get this level of done-ness and still make quick progress from iteration to iteration? You create a set of automated tests that, when they pass, meet all of the above criteria! When the acceptance tests for your feature pass, you are *done*.

Professional developers drive the definition of their requirements all the way to automated acceptance tests. They work with stakeholder's and QA to ensure that these automated tests are a complete specification of done.

Sam: "OK, now these log files need to be backed up."

Paula: "OK, how often?"

Sam: "Daily."

Paula: "Right. And where do you want it saved?"

Sam: "What do you mean?"

Paula: "Do you want me to save it a particular sub-directory?"

Sam: "Yes, that'd be good."

Paula: "What shall we call it?"

Sam: "How about 'backup'"?

Tom (tester): "Wait, backup is too common a name. What are you really storing in this directory?"

Sam: "The backups."

Tom: "Backups of what?"

Sam: "The log files."

Paula: "But there's only one log file."

Sam: "No, there are many. One for each day."

Tom: "You mean that there is one *active* log file, and many log file backups?"

Sam: "Of course."

Paula: "Oh! I thought you just wanted a temporary backup."

Sam: "No, the customer wants to keep them all forever."

Paula: "That's a new one on me. OK, glad we cleared that up."

Tom: "So the name of the sub-directory should tell us exactly what's in it."

Sam: "It's got all the old inactive logs."

Tom: "So let's call it `old_inactive_logs`."

Sam: "Great."

Tom: "So when does this directory get created?"

Sam: "Huh?"

Paula: "We should create the directory when the system starts, but only if the directory doesn't already exist."

Tom: "OK, there's our first test. I'll need to start up the system and see if the `old_inactive_logs` directory is created. Then I'll add a file to that directory. Then I'll shut down, and start again, and make sure both the directory and the file are still there."

Paula: "That test is going to take you a long time to run. System start-up is already 20 seconds, and growing. Besides, I really don't want to have to build the whole system every time I run the acceptance tests."

Tom: "What do you suggest?"

Paula: "We'll create a `SystemStarter` class. The main program will load this starter with a group of `StartupCommand` objects, which will follow the COMMAND pattern. Then during system start-up the `SystemStarter` will simply tell all the `StartupCommand` objects to run. One of those `StartupCommand` derivatives will create the `old_inactive_logs` directory, but only if it doesn't already exist."

Tom: "Oh, OK, then all I need to test is that `StartupCommand` derivative. I can write a simple FITNESSE test for that."

Tom goes to the board.

"The first part will look something like this":

```
given the command LogFileDirectoryStartupCommand
given that the old_inactive_logs directory does not exist
```

```
when the command is executed
then the old_inactive_logs directory should exist
and it should be empty
```

"The second part will look like this":

```
given the command LogFileDirectoryStartupCommand
given that the old_inactive_logs directory exists
and that it contains a file named x
When the command is executed
Then the old_inactive_logs directory should still exist
and it should still contain a file named x
```

Paula: "Yeah, that should cover it."

Sam: "Wow, is all that really necessary?"

Paula: "Sam, which of these two statements isn't important enough to specify?"

Sam: "I just mean that it looks like a lot of work to think up and write all these tests."

Tom: "It is, but it's no more work than writing a manual test plan. And it's *much* more work to repeatedly execute a manual test."

COMMUNICATION

The purpose of acceptance tests is communication, clarity, and precision. By agreeing to them, the developers, stakeholders, and testers all understand what the plan for the system behavior is. Achieving this kind of clarity is the responsibility of all parties. Professional developers make it their responsibility to work with stakeholders and testers to ensure that all parties know what is about to be built.

AUTOMATION

Acceptance tests should *always* be automated. There is a place for manual testing elsewhere in the software lifecycle, but *these* kinds of tests should never be manual. The reason is simple: cost.

Consider the image in Figure 7-1. The hands you see there belong to the QA manager of a large Internet company. The document he is holding is the *table of contents* for his *manual* test plan. He has an army of manual testers in off-shore locations that execute this plan once every six weeks. It costs him over a million dollars every time. He's holding it out for me because he's just come back from a meeting in which his manager has told him that they need to cut his budget by 50%. His question to me is, "Which half of these tests should I not run?"

Figure 7-1 Manual test plan

To call this a disaster would be a gross understatement. The cost of running the manual test plan is so enormous that they have decided to sacrifice it and simply live with the fact that *they won't know if half of their product works!*

Professional developers do not let this kind of situation happen. The cost of automating acceptance tests is so small in comparison to the cost of executing manual test plans that it makes no economic sense to write scripts for humans to execute. Professional developers take responsibility for their part in ensuring that acceptance tests are automated.

There are many open-source and commercial tools that facilitate the automation of acceptance tests. FITNESSE, Cucumber, cuke4duke, robot framework, and Selenium, just to mention a few. All these tools allow you to specify automated tests in a form that nonprogrammers can read, understand, and even author.

EXTRA WORK

Sam's point about work is understandable. It *does* look like a lot of extra work to write acceptance tests like this. But given Figure 7-1 we can see that it's not really extra work at all. Writing these tests is simply the work of specifying the system. Specifying at this level of detail is the only way we, as programmers, can know what "done" means. Specifying at this level of detail is the only way that the stakeholders can ensure that the system they are paying for really does what they need. And specifying at this level of detail is the only way to successfully automate the tests. So don't look at these tests as extra work. Look at them as massive time and money savers. These tests will prevent you from implementing the wrong system and will allow you to *know* when you are done.

WHO WRITES ACCEPTANCE TESTS, AND WHEN?

In an ideal world, the stakeholders and QA would collaborate to write these tests, and developers would review them for consistency. In the real world, stakeholders seldom have the time or inclination to dive into the required level of detail. So they often delegate the responsibility to business analysts, QA, or even developers. If it turns out that developers must write these tests, then take care that the developer who writes the test is not the same as the developer who implements the tested feature.

Typically business analysts write the "happy path" versions of the tests, because those tests describe the features that have business value. QA typically writes the "unhappy path" tests, the boundary conditions, exceptions, and corner cases. This is because QA's job is to help think about what can go wrong.

Following the principle of "late precision," acceptance tests should be written as late as possible, typically a few days before the feature is implemented. In Agile projects, the tests are written *after* the features have been selected for the next Iteration or Sprint.

The first few acceptance tests should be ready by the first day of the iteration. More should be completed each day until the midpoint of the iteration when all of them should be ready. If all the acceptance tests aren't ready by the midpoint of the iteration, then some developers will have to pitch in to finish them off. If this happens frequently, then more BAs and/or QAs should be added to the team.

THE DEVELOPER'S ROLE

Implementation work on a feature begins when the acceptance tests for that feature are ready. The developers execute the acceptance tests for the new feature and see how they fail. Then they work to connect the acceptance test to the system, and then start making the test pass by implementing the desired feature.

> Paula: "Peter, would you give me a hand with this story?"
>
> Peter: "Sure, Paula, what's up?"
>
> Paula: "Here's the acceptance test. As you can see, it's failing."

```
given the command LogFileDirectoryStartupCommand
given that the old_inactive_logs directory does not exist
when the command is executed
then the old_inactive_logs directory should exist
and it should be empty
```

> Peter: "Yeah, all red. None of the scenarios are written. Let me write the first one."

```
|scenario|given the command _|cmd|
|create command|@cmd|
```

> Paula: "Do we already have a createCommand operation?"
>
> Peter: "Yeah, it's in the CommandUtilitiesFixture that I wrote last week."
>
> Paula: "OK, so let's run the test now."
>
> Peter: (runs test). "Yeah, the first line is green, let's move on to the next."

Don't worry too much about Scenarios and Fixtures. Those are just some of the plumbing you have to write to connect the tests to the system being tested.

Suffice it to say that the tools all provide some way to use pattern matching to recognize and parse the statements of the test, and then to call functions that feed the data in the test into the system being tested. The amount of effort is small, and the Scenarios and Fixtures are reusable across many different tests.

The point of all this is that it is the developer's job to connect the acceptance tests to the system, and then to make those tests pass.

TEST NEGOTIATION AND PASSIVE AGGRESSION

Test authors are human and make mistakes. Sometimes the tests as written don't make a lot of sense once you start implementing them. They might be too complicated. They might be awkward. They might contains silly assumptions. Or they might just be wrong. This can be very frustrating if you are the developer who has to make the test pass.

As a professional developer, it is your job to negotiate with the test author for a better test. What you should *never* do is take the passive-aggressive option and say to yourself, "Well, that's what the test says, so that's what I'm going to do."

Remember, as a professional it is your job to help your team create the best software they can. That means that everybody needs to watch out for errors and slip-ups, and work together to correct them.

Paula: "Tom, this test isn't quite right."

```
ensure that the post operation finishes in 2 seconds.
```

Tom: "It looks OK to me. Our requirement is that users should not have to wait more than two seconds. What's the problem?"

Paula: "The problem is we can only make that guarantee in a statistical sense."

Tom: "Huh? That sounds like weasel words. The requirement is two seconds."

Paula: "Right, and we can achieve that 99.5% of the time."

Tom: "Paula, that's not the requirement."

Paula: "But it's reality. There's no way I can make the guarantee any other way."

Tom: "Sam's going to throw a fit."

Paula: "No, actually, I've already spoken to him about it. He's fine as long as the *normal* user experience is two seconds or less."

Tom: "OK, so how do I write this test? I can't just say that the post operation *usually* finishes in two seconds."

Paula: "You say it statistically."

Tom: "You mean you want me to run a thousand post operation and make sure no more than five are more than two seconds? That's absurd."

Paula: "No, that would take the better part of an hour to run. How about this?"

```
execute 15 post transactions and accumulate times.
ensure that the Z score for 2 seconds is at least 2.57
```

Tom: "Whoa, what's a Z score?"

Paula: "Just a bit of statistics. Here, how about this?"

```
execute 15 post transactions and accumulate times.
ensure odds are 99.5% that time will be less than 2 seconds.
```

Tom: "Yeah, that's readable, sort of, but can I trust the math behind the scenes?"

Paula: "I'll make sure to show all the intermediate calculations in the test report so that you can check the math if you have any doubts."

Tom: "OK, that works for me."

ACCEPTANCE TESTS AND UNIT TESTS

Acceptance tests are not *unit* tests. Unit tests are written *by* programmers *for* programmers. They are formal design documents that describe the lowest level structure and behavior of the code. The audience is programmers, not business.

Acceptance tests are written *by* the business *for* the business (even when you, the developer, end up writing them). They are formal requirements documents that specify how the system should behave from the business' point of view. The audience is the business *and* the programmers.

It can be tempting to try to eliminate "extra work" by assuming that the two kinds of tests are redundant. Although it is true that unit and acceptance tests often test the same things, they are not redundant at all.

First, although they may test the same things, they do so through different mechanisms and pathways. Unit tests dig into the guts of the system making calls to methods in particular classes. Acceptance tests invoke the system much farther out, at the API or sometimes even UI level. So the execution pathways that these tests take are very different.

But the real reason these tests aren't redundant is that their primary function *is not testing*. The fact that they are tests is incidental. Unit tests and acceptance tests are documents first, and tests second. Their primary purpose is to formally document the design, structure, and behavior of the system. The fact that they automatically verify the design, structure, and behavior that they specify is wildly useful, but the specification is their true purpose.

GUIs AND OTHER COMPLICATIONS

It is hard to specify GUIs up front. It can be done, but it is seldom done well. The reason is that the aesthetics are subjective and therefore volatile. People want to *fiddle* with GUIs. They want to massage and manipulate them. They want to try different fonts, colors, page-layouts, and workflows. GUIs are constantly in flux.

This makes it challenging to write acceptance tests for GUIs. The trick is to design the system so that you can treat the GUI as though it were an API rather than a set of buttons, sliders, grids, and menus. This may sound strange, but it's really just good design.

There is a design principle called the Single Responsibility Principle (SRP). This principle states that you should separate those things that change for different reasons, and group together those things that change for the same reasons. GUIs are no exception.

The layout, format, and workflow of the GUI will change for aesthetic and efficiency reasons, but the underlying capability of the GUI will remain the same despite these changes. Therefore, when writing acceptance tests for a GUI you take advantage of the underlying abstractions that don't change very frequently.

For example, there may be several buttons on a page. Rather than creating tests that click on those buttons based on their positions on the page, you may be able to click on them based on their names. Better yet, perhaps they each have a unique ID that you can use. It is much better to write a test that selects the button whose ID is ok_button than it is to select the button in column 3 of row 4 of the control grid.

Testing through the Right Interface

Better still is to write tests that invoke the features of the underlying system through a real API rather than through the GUI. This API should be the same API used by the GUI. This is nothing new. Design experts have been telling us for decades to separate our GUIs from our business rules.

Testing through the GUI is always problematic unless you are testing *just* the GUI. The reason is that the GUI is likely to change, making the tests very fragile. When every GUI change breaks a thousand tests, you are either going to start throwing the tests away or you are going to stop changing the GUI. Neither of those are good options. So write your business rule tests to go through an API just below the GUI.

Some acceptance tests specify the behavior of the GUI itself. These tests *must* go through the GUI. However, these tests do not test business rules and therefore don't require the business rules to be connected to the GUI. Therefore, it is a good idea to decouple the GUI and the business rules and replace the business rules with stubs while testing the GUI itself.

Keep the GUI tests to a minimum. They are fragile, because the GUI is volatile. The more GUI tests you have the less likely you are to keep them.

CONTINUOUS INTEGRATION

Make sure that all your unit tests and acceptance tests are run several times per day in a *continuous integration* system. This system should be triggered by your source code control system. Every time someone commits a module, the CI system should kick off a build, and then run all the tests in the system. The results of that run should be emailed to everyone on the team.

Stop the Presses

It is very important to keep the CI tests running at all times. They should never fail. If they fail, then the whole team should stop what they are doing and focus on getting the broken tests to pass again. A broken build in the CI system should be viewed as an emergency, a "stop the presses" event.

I have consulted for teams that failed to take broken tests seriously. They were "too busy" to fix the broken tests so they set them aside, promising to fix them later. In one case the team actually took the broken tests out of the build because it was so inconvenient to see them fail. Later, after releasing to the customer, they realized that they had forgotten to put those tests back into the build. They learned this because an angry customer was calling them with bug reports.

CONCLUSION

Communication about details is hard. This is especially true for programmers and stakeholders communicating about the details of an application. It is too easy for each party to wave their hands and *assume* that the other party understands. All too often both parties agree that they understand and leave with completely different ideas.

The only way I know of to effectively eliminate communication errors between programmers and stakeholders is to write automated acceptance tests. These tests are so formal that they execute. They are completely unambiguous, and they cannot get out of sync with the application. They are the perfect requirements document.

TESTING 8 STRATEGIES

Professional developers test their code. But testing is not simply a matter of writing a few unit tests or a few acceptance tests. Writing these tests is a good thing, but it is far from sufficient. What every professional development team needs is a good *testing strategy*.

In 1989, I was working at Rational on the first release of Rose. Every month or so our QA manager would call a "Bug Hunt" day. Everyone on the team, from programmers to managers to secretaries to database administrators, would sit down with Rose and try to make it fail. Prizes were awarded for various types of bugs. The person who found a crashing bug could win a dinner for two. The person who found the most bugs might win a weekend in Monterrey.

QA SHOULD FIND NOTHING

I've said this before, and I'll say it again. Despite the fact that your company may have a separate QA group to test the software, it should be the goal of the development group that QA find nothing wrong.

Of course, it's not likely that this goal will be constantly achieved. After all, when you have a group of intelligent people bound and determined to find all the wrinkles and deficits in a product, they are likely going to find some. Still, every time QA finds something the development team should react in horror. They should ask themselves how it happened and take steps to prevent it in the future.

QA IS PART OF THE TEAM

The previous section might have made it seem that QA and Development are at odds with each other, that their relationship is adversarial. This is not the intent. Rather, QA and Development should be working together to ensure the quality of the system. The best role for the QA part of the team is to act as specifiers and characterizers.

QA as Specifiers

It should be QA's role to work with business to create the automated acceptance tests that become the true specification and requirements document for the system. Iteration by iteration they gather the requirements from business and translate them into tests that describe to developers how the system should behave (See Chapter 7, "Acceptance Testing"). In general, the business writes the happy-path tests, while QA writes the corner, boundary, and unhappy-path tests.

QA as Characterizers

The other role for QA is to use the discipline of exploratory testing[1] to characterize the true behavior of the running system and report that behavior

---

1. http://www.satisfice.com/articles/what_is_et.shtml

back to development and business. In this role QA is *not* interpreting the requirements. Rather, they are identifying the actual behaviors of the system.

THE TEST AUTOMATION PYRAMID

Professional developers employ the discipline of Test Driven Development to create unit tests. Professional development teams use acceptance tests to specify their system, and continuous integration (Chapter 7, page 110) to prevent regression. But these tests are only part of the story. As good as it is to have a suite of unit and acceptance tests, we also need higher-level tests to ensure that QA finds nothing. Figure 8-1 shows the Test Automation Pyramid,[2] a graphical depiction of the kinds of tests that a professional development organization needs.

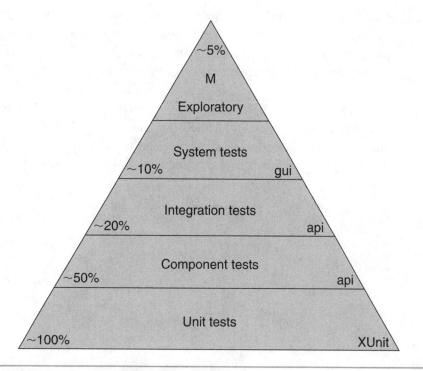

Figure 8-1 The test automation pyramid

2. [COHN09] pp. 311–312

Unit Tests

At the bottom of the pyramid are the unit tests. These tests are written by programmers, for programmers, in the programming language of the system. The intent of these tests is to specify the system at the lowest level. Developers write these tests before writing production code as a way to specify what they are about to write. They are executed as part of Continuous Integration to ensure that the intent of the programmers' is upheld.

Unit tests provide as close to 100% coverage as is practical. Generally this number should be somewhere in the 90s. And it should be *true* coverage as opposed to false tests that execute code without asserting its behavior.

Component Tests

These are some of the acceptance tests mentioned in the previous chapter. Generally they are written against individual components of the system. The components of the system encapsulate the business rules, so the tests for those components are the acceptance tests for those business rules

As depicted in Figure 8-2 a component test wraps a component. It passes input data into the component and gathers output data from it. It tests that the output matches the input. Any other system components are decoupled from the test using appropriate mocking and test-doubling techniques.

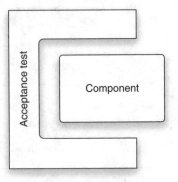

Figure 8-2 Component acceptance test

Component tests are written by QA and Business with assistance from development. They are composed in a component-testing environment such as FitNesse, JBehave, or Cucumber. (GUI components are tested with GUI testing environments such as Selenium or Watir.) The intent is that the business should be able to read and interpret these tests, if not author them.

Component tests cover roughly half the system. They are directed more towards happy-path situations and very obvious corner, boundary, and alternate-path cases. The vast majority of unhappy-path cases are covered by unit tests and are meaningless at the level of component tests.

INTEGRATION TESTS

These tests only have meaning for larger systems that have many components. As shown in Figure 8-3, these tests assemble groups of components and test how well they communicate with each other. The other components of the system are decoupled as usual with appropriate mocks and test-doubles.

Integration tests are *choreography* tests. They do not test business rules. Rather, they test how well the assembly of components dances together. They are *plumbing* tests that make sure that the components are properly connected and can clearly communicate with each other.

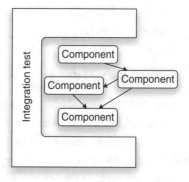

Figure 8-3 Integration test

Integration tests are typically written by the system architects, or lead designers, of the system. The tests ensure that the architectural structure of the system is sound. It is at this level that we might see performance and throughput tests.

Integration tests are typically written in the same language and environment as component tests. They are typically *not* executed as part of the Continuous Integration suite, because they often have longer runtimes. Instead, these tests are run periodically (nightly, weekly, etc.) as deemed necessary by their authors.

SYSTEM TESTS

These are automated tests that execute against the entire integrated system. They are the ultimate integration tests. They do not test business rules directly. Rather, they test that the system has been wired together correctly and its parts interoperate according to plan. We would expect to see throughput and performance tests in this suite.

These tests are written by the system architects and technical leads. Typically they are written in the same language and environment as integration tests for the UI. They are executed relatively infrequently depending on their duration, but the more frequently the better.

System tests cover perhaps 10% of the system. This is because their intent is not to ensure correct system behavior, but correct system *construction*. The correct behavior of the underlying code and components have already been ascertained by the lower layers of the pyramid.

MANUAL EXPLORATORY TESTS

This is where humans put their hands on the keyboards and their eyes on the screens. These tests are not automated, *nor are they scripted*. The intent of these tests is to explore the system for unexpected behaviors while confirming expected behaviors. Toward that end we need human brains, with human creativity, working to investigate and explore the system. Creating a written test plan for this kind of testing defeats the purpose.

Some teams will have specialists do this work. Other teams will simply declare a day or two of "bug hunting" in which as many people as possible, including managers, secretaries, programmers, testers, and tech writers, "bang" on the system to see if they can make it break.

The goal is not coverage. We are not going to prove out every business rule and every execution pathway with these tests. Rather, the goal is to ensure that the system behaves well under human operation and to creatively find as many "peculiarities" as possible.

CONCLUSION

TDD is a powerful discipline, and Acceptance Tests are valuable ways to express and enforce requirements. But they are only part of a total testing strategy. To make good on the goal that "QA should find nothing," development teams need to work hand in hand with QA to create a hierarchy of unit, component, integration, system, and exploratory tests. These tests should be run as frequently as possible to provide maximum feedback and to ensure that the system remains continuously clean.

BIBLIOGRAPHY

[**COHN09**]: Mike Cohn, *Succeeding with Agile,* Boston, MA: Addison-Wesley, 2009.

TIME MANAGEMENT

Eight hours is a remarkably short period of time. It's just 480 minutes or 28,800 seconds. As a professional, you expect that you will use those few precious seconds as efficiently and effectively as possible. What strategy can you use to ensure that you don't waste the little time you have? How can you effectively manage your time?

In 1986 I was living in Little Sandhurst, Surrey, England. I was managing a 15-person software development department for Teradyne in Bracknell. My days were hectic with phone calls, impromptu meetings, field service issues, and interruptions. So in order to get any work done I had to adopt some pretty drastic time-management disciplines.

- I awoke at 5 every morning and rode my bicycle to the office in Bracknell by 6 AM. That gave me 2-$\frac{1}{2}$ hours of quiet time before the chaos of the day began.
- Upon arrival I would write a schedule on my board. I divided time into 15-minute increments and filled in the activity I would work on during that block of time.
- I completely filled the first 3 hours of that schedule. Starting at 9 AM I started leaving one 15-minute gap per hour; that way I could quickly push most interruptions into one of those open slots and continue working.
- I left the time after lunch unscheduled because I knew that by then all hell would have broken loose and I'd have to be in reactive mode for the rest of the day. During those rare afternoon periods that the chaos did not intrude, I simply worked on the most important thing until it did.

This scheme did not always succeed. Waking up at 5 AM was not always feasible, and sometimes the chaos broke through all my careful strategies and consumed my day. But for the most part I was able to keep my head above water.

MEETINGS

Meetings cost about $200 per hour per attendee. This takes into account salaries, benefits, facilities costs, and so forth. The next time you are in a meeting, calculate the cost. You may be amazed.

There are two truths about meeting.

1. Meetings are necessary.
2. Meetings are huge time wasters.

Often these two truths equally describe the same meeting. Some in attendance may find them invaluable; others may find them redundant or useless.

Professionals are aware of the high cost of meetings. They are also aware that their own time is precious; they have code to write and schedules to meet. Therefore, they actively resist attending meetings that don't have an immediate and significant benefit.

DECLINING

You do not have to attend every meeting to which you are invited. Indeed, it is unprofessional to go to too many meetings. You need to use your time wisely. So be very careful about which meetings you attend and which you politely refuse.

The person inviting you to a meeting is not responsible for managing your time. Only *you* can do that. So when you receive a meeting invitation, don't accept unless it is a meeting for which your participation is immediately and significantly necessary to the job you are doing now.

Sometimes the meeting will be about something that interests you, but is not immediately necessary. You will have to choose whether you can afford the time. Be careful—there may be more than enough of these meetings to consume your days.

Sometimes the meeting will be about something that you can contribute to but is not immediately significant to what you are currently doing. You will have to choose whether the loss to your project is worth the benefit to theirs. This may sound cynical, but your responsibility is to *your* projects first. Still, it is often good for one team to help another, so you may want to discuss your participation with your team and manager.

Sometimes your presence at the meeting will be requested by someone in authority, such as a very senior engineer in another project or the manager of a different project. You will have to choose whether that authority outweighs your work schedule. Again, your team and your supervisor can be of help in making that decision.

One of the most important duties of your manager is to keep you *out* of meetings. A good manager will be more than willing to defend your decision to decline attendance because that manager is just as concerned about your time as you are.

LEAVING

Meetings don't always go as planned. Sometimes you find yourself sitting in a meeting that you would have declined had you known more. Sometimes new topics get added, or somebody's pet peeve dominates the discussion. Over the years I've developed a simple rule: When the meeting gets boring, leave.

Again, you have an obligation to manage your time well. If you find yourself stuck in a meeting that is not a good use of your time, you need to find a way to politely exit that meeting.

Clearly you should not storm out of a meeting exclaiming "This is boring!" There's no need to be rude. You can simply ask, at an opportune moment, if your presence is still necessary. You can explain that you can't afford a lot more time, and ask whether there is a way to expedite the discussion or shuffle the agenda.

The important thing to realize is that remaining in a meeting that has become a waste of time for you, and to which you can no longer significantly contribute, is unprofessional. You have an obligation to wisely spend your employer's time and money, so it is not unprofessional to choose an appropriate moment to negotiate your exit.

HAVE AN AGENDA AND A GOAL

The reason we are willing to endure the cost of meetings is that we sometimes *do* need the participants together in a room to help achieve a specific goal. To use the participants' time wisely, the meeting should have a clear agenda, with times for each topic and a stated goal.

If you are asked to go to a meeting, make sure you know what discussions are on the table, how much time is allotted for them, and what goal is to be achieved. If you can't get a clear answer on these things, then politely decline to attend.

If you go to a meeting and you find that the agenda has been high-jacked or abandoned, you should request that the new topic be tabled and the agenda be followed. If this doesn't happen, you should politely leave when possible.

Stand-Up Meetings

These meetings are part of the Agile cannon. Their name comes from the fact that the participants are expected to stand while the meeting is in session. Each participant takes a turn to answer three questions:

1. What did I do yesterday?
2. What am I going to do today?
3. What's in my way?

That's all. Each question should require *no more than* twenty seconds, so each participant should require no more than one minute. Even in a group of ten people this meeting should be over well before ten minutes has elapsed.

Iteration Planning Meetings

These are the most difficult meetings in the Agile canon to do well. Done poorly, they take far too much time. It takes skill to make these meetings go well, a skill that is well worth learning.

Iteration planning meetings are meant to select the backlog items that will be executed in the next iteration. Estimates should already be done for the candidate items. Assessment of business value should already be done. In really good organizations the acceptance/component tests will already be written, or at least sketched out.

The meeting should proceed quickly with each candidate backlog item being briefly discussed and then either selected or rejected. No more than five or ten minutes should be spent on any given item. If a longer discussion is needed, it should be scheduled for another time with a subset of the team.

My rule of thumb is that the meeting should take no more than 5% of the total time in the iteration. So for a one week iteration (forty hours) the meeting should be over within two hours.

ITERATION RESTROSPECTIVE AND DEMO

These meetings are conducted at the end of each iteration. Team members discuss what went right and what went wrong. Stakeholders see a demo of the newly working features. These meetings can be badly abused and can soak up a lot of time, so schedule them 45 minutes before quitting time on the last day of the iteration. Allocate no more than 20 minutes for retrospective and 25 minutes for the demo. Remember, it's only been a week or two so there shouldn't be all that much to talk about.

ARGUMENTS/DISAGREEMENTS

Kent Beck once told me something profound: "Any argument that can't be settled in five minutes can't be settled by arguing." The reason it goes on so long is that there is no clear evidence supporting either side. The argument is probably religious, as opposed to factual.

Technical disagreements tend to go off into the stratosphere. Each party has all kinds of justifications for their position but seldom any data. Without data, any argument that doesn't forge agreement within a few minutes (somewhere between five and thirty) simply won't ever forge agreement. The only thing to do is to go get some data.

Some folks will try to win an argument by force of character. They might yell, or get in your face, or act condescending. It doesn't matter; force of will doesn't settle disagreements for long. Data does.

Some folks will be passive-aggressive. They'll agree just to end the argument, and then sabotage the result by refusing to engage in the solution. They'll say to themselves, "This is the way they wanted it, and now they're going to get what they wanted." This is probably the worst kind of unprofessional behavior there is. Never, ever do this. If you agree, then you *must* engage.

How do you get the data you need to settle a disagreement? Sometimes you can run experiments, or do some simulation or modeling. But sometimes the best alternative is to simply flip a coin to choose one of the two paths in question.

If things work out, then that path was workable. If you get into trouble, you can back out and go down the other path. It would be wise to agree on a time as well as a set of criteria to help determine when the chosen path should be abandoned.

Beware of meetings that are really just a venue to vent a disagreement and to gather support for one side or the other. And avoid those where only one of the arguers is presenting.

If an argument must truly be settled, then ask each of the arguers to present their case to the team in five minutes or less. Then have the team vote. The whole meeting will take less than fifteen minutes.

FOCUS-MANNA

Forgive me if this section seems to smell of New Age metaphysics, or perhaps of Dungeons & Dragons. It's just that this is the way I think about this topic.

Programming is an intellectual exercise that requires extended periods of concentration and focus. Focus is a scarce resource, rather like manna.[1] After you have expended your focus-manna, you have to recharge by doing unfocused activities for an hour or more.

I don't know what this focus-manna is, but I have a feeling that it is a physical substance (or possibly its lack) that affects alterness and attention. Whatever it may be, you can *feel* when it's there, and you can feel when it's gone. Professional developers learn to manage their time to take advantage of their focus-manna. We write code when our focus-manna is high; and we do other, less productive things when it's not.

Focus-manna is also a decaying resource. If you don't use it when it's there, you are likely to lose it. That's one of the reasons that meetings can be so

---

1. Manna is a common commodity in fantasy and role-playing games like Dungeons & Dragons. Every player has a certain amount of manna, which is a magical substance expended whenever a player casts a magical spell. The more potent the spell, the more of that player's manna is consumed. Manna recharges at a slow, fixed daily rate. So it's easy to use it all up in a few spell-casting sessions.

devastating. If you spend all your focus-manna in a meeting, you won't have any left for coding.

Worry and distractions also consume focus-manna. The fight you had with your spouse last night, the dent you put in your fender this morning, or the bill you forgot to pay last week will all suck the focus-manna out of you quickly.

SLEEP

I can't stress this one strongly enough. I have the most focus-manna after a good night's sleep. Seven hours of sleep will often give me a full eight hours' worth of focus-manna. Professional developers manage their sleep schedule to ensure that they have topped up their focus-manna by the time they get to work in the morning.

CAFFEINE

There is no doubt that some of us can make more efficient use of our focus-manna by consuming moderate amounts of caffeine. But take care. Caffeine also puts a strange "jitter" on your focus. Too much of it can send your focus off in very strange directions. A really strong caffeine buzz can cause you to waste an entire day hyper-focussing on all the wrong things.

Caffeine usage and tolerance is a personal thing. My personal preference is a single strong cup of coffee in the morning and a diet coke with lunch. I sometimes double this dose, but seldom do more than that.

RECHARGING

Focus-manna can be partially recharged by de-focussing. A good long walk, a conversation with friends, a time of just looking out a window can all help to pump the focus-manna back up.

Some people meditate. Other people grab a power nap. Others will listen to a podcast or thumb through a magazine.

I have found that once the manna is gone, you can't force the focus. You can still write code, but you'll almost certainly have to rewrite it the next day, or live with a rotting mass for weeks or months. So it's better to take thirty, or even sixty minutes to de-focus.

Muscle Focus

There is something peculiar about doing physical disciplines such as martial arts, tai-chi or yoga. Even though these activities require significant focus, it is a different kind of focus from coding. It's not intellectual, it's muscle. And somehow muscle focus helps to recharge mental focus. It's more than a simple recharge though. I find that a regular regimen of muscle focus increases my capacity for mental focus.

My chosen form of physical focus is bike riding. I'll ride for an hour or two, sometimes covering twenty or thirty miles. I ride on a trail that parallels the Des Plaines river, so I don't have to deal with cars.

While I ride I listen to podcasts about astronomy or politics. Sometimes I just listen to my favorite music. And sometimes I just turn the headphones off and listen to nature.

Some people take the time to work with their hands. Perhaps they enjoy carpentry, or building models, or gardening. Whatever the activity, there is something about activities that focus on muscles that enhances the ability to work with your mind.

Input versus Output

Another thing I find essential for focus is to balance my output with appropriate input. Writing software is a *creative* exercise. I find that I am most creative when I am exposed to other people's creativity. So I read lots of science fiction. The creativity of those authors somehow stimulates my own creative juices for software.

TIME BOXING AND TOMATOES

One very effective way that I've used to manage my time and focus is to use the well-known Pomodoro Technique,[2] otherwise knows as *tomatoes*. The basic idea is very simple. You set a standard kitchen timer (traditionally shaped like a tomato) for 25 minutes. While that timer is running, you let *nothing* interfere with what you are doing. If the phone rings you answer and politely ask if you can call back within 25 minutes. If someone stops in to ask you a question you politely ask if you can get back to them within 25 minutes. Regardless of the interruption, you simply defer it until the timer dings. After all, few interruptions are so horribly urgent that they can't wait 25 minutes!

When the tomato timer dings you stop what you are doing *immediately*. You deal with any interruptions that occurred during the tomato. Then you take a break of five minutes or so. Then you set the timer for another 25 minutes and start the next tomato. Every fourth tomato you take a longer break of 30 minutes or so.

There is quite a bit written about this technique, and I urge you to read it. However, the description above should provide you with the gist of the technique.

Using this technique your time is divided into tomato and non-tomato time. Tomato time is productive. It is within tomatoes that you get real work done. Time outside of tomatoes is either distractions, meetings, breaks, or other time that is not spent working on your tasks.

How many tomatoes can you get done in a day? On a good day you might get 12 or even 14 tomatoes done. On a bad day, you might only get two or three done. If you count them, and chart them, you'll get a pretty quick feel for how much of your day you spend productive and how much you spend dealing with "stuff."

Some people get so comfortable with the technique that they estimate their tasks in tomatoes and then measure their weekly tomato velocity. But this is just icing on the cake. The real benefit of the Pomodoro Technique is that 25-minute window of productive time that you aggressively defend against all interruptions.

---

2. http://www.pomodorotechnique.com/

AVOIDANCE

Sometimes your heart just isn't in your work. It may be that the thing that needs doing is scary or uncomfortable or boring. Perhaps you think it will force you into a confrontation or lead you into an inescapable rat hole. Or maybe you just plain don't want to do it.

PRIORITY INVERSION

Whatever the reason, you find ways to avoid doing the real work. You convince yourself that something else is more urgent, and you do that instead. This is called *priority inversion.* You raise the priority of a task so that you can postpone the task that has the true priority. Priority inversions are a lie we tell ourselves. We can't face what needs to be done, so we convince ourselves that another task is more important. We know it's not, but we lie to ourselves.

Actually, we aren't lying to ourselves. What we are really doing is preparing for the lie we'll tell when someone asks us what we are doing and why we are doing it. We are building a defense to protect us from the judgment of others.

Clearly this is unprofessional behavior. Professionals evaluate the priority of each task, disregarding their personal fears and desires, and execute those tasks in priority order.

BLIND ALLEYS

Blind alleys are a fact of life for all software craftsmen. Sometimes you will make a decision and wander down a technical pathway that leads to nowhere. The more vested you are in your decision, the longer you will wander in the wilderness. If you've staked your professional reputation, you'll wander forever.

Prudence and experience will help you avoid certain blind alleys, but you'll never avoid them all. So the real skill you need is to quickly realize when you are in one, and have the courage to back out. This is sometimes called *The Rule of Holes:* When you are in one, stop digging.

Professionals avoid getting so vested in an idea that they can't abandon it and turn around. They keep an open mind about other ideas so that when they hit a dead end they still have other options.

MARSHES, BOGS, SWAMPS, AND OTHER MESSES

Worse than blind alleys are messes. Messes slow you down, but don't stop you. Messes impede your progress, but you can still make progress through sheer brute force. Messes are worse than blind alleys because you can always see the way forward, and it always looks shorter than the way back (but it isn't).

I have seen products ruined and companies destroyed by software messes. I've seen the productivity of teams decrease from jitterbug to dirge in just a few months. Nothing has a more profound or long-lasting negative effect on the productivity of a software team than a mess. Nothing.

The problem is that starting a mess, like going down a blind alley, is unavoidable. Experience and prudence can help you to avoid them, but eventually you will make a decision that leads to a mess.

The progression of such a mess is insidious. You create a solution to a simple problem, being careful to keep the code simple and clean. As the problem grows in scope and complexity you extend that code base, keeping it as clean as you can. At some point you realize that you made a wrong design choice when you started, and that your code doesn't scale well in the direction that the requirements are moving.

This is the inflection point! You can still go back and fix the design. But you can also continue to go forward. Going back looks expensive because you'll have to rework the existing code, but going back will *never* be easier than it is now. If you go forward you will drive the system into a swamp from which it may never escape.

Professionals fear messes far more than they fear blind alleys. They are always on the lookout for messes that start to grow without bound, and will expend all necessary effort to escape from them as early and as quickly as possible.

Moving forward through a swamp, when you *know* it's a swamp, is the worst kind of priority inversion. By moving forward you are lying to yourself, lying to your team, lying to your company, and lying to your customers. You are telling them that all will be well, when in fact you are heading to a shared doom.

CONCLUSION

Software professionals are diligent in the management of their time and their focus. They understand the temptations of priority inversion and fight it as a matter of honor. They keep their options open by keeping an open mind about alternate solutions. They never become so vested in a solution that they can't abandon it. And they are always on the lookout for growing messes, and they clean them as soon as they are recognized. There is no sadder sight than a team of software developers fruitlessly slogging through an ever-deepening bog.

ESTIMATION 10

Estimation is one of the simplest, yet most frightening activities that software professionals face. So much business value depends on it. So much of our reputations ride on it. So much of our angst and failure are caused by it. It is the primary wedge that has been driven between business people and developers. It is the source of nearly all the distrust that rules that relationship.

In 1978, I was the lead developer for a 32K embedded Z-80 program written in assembly language. The program was burned onto 32 1K × 8 EEprom chips. These 32 chips were inserted into three boards, each of which held 12 chips.

We had hundreds of devices in the field, installed in telephone central offices all over the United States. Whenever we fixed a bug or added a feature, we'd have to send field service techs to each of those units and have them replace all 32 chips!

This was a nightmare. The chips and the boards were fragile. The pins on the chips could bend and break. The constant flexing of the boards could damage solder joints. The risk of breakage and error were enormous. The cost to the company was far too high.

My boss, Ken Finder, came to me and asked me to fix this. What he wanted was a way to make a change to a chip that did not require all the other chips to change. If you've read my books, or heard my talks, you know I rant a lot about independent deployability. This is where I first learned that lesson.

Our problem was that the software was a single linked executable. If a new line of code was added to the program, all the addresses of the following lines of code changed. Since each chip simply held 1K of the address space, the contents of virtually all the chips would change.

The solution was pretty simple. Each chip had to be decoupled from all the others. Each had to be turned into an independent compilation unit that could be burned independently of all the others.

So I measured the sizes of all the functions in the application and wrote a simple program that fit them, like a jigsaw puzzle, into each of the chips, leaving 100 bytes of space or so for expansion. At the beginning of each chip I put a table of pointers to all the functions on that chip. At boot-up these pointers were moved into RAM. All the code in the system was changed so that functions were called only through these RAM vectors and never directly.

Yes, you got it. The chips were objects, with vtables. All functions were poly-morphically deployed. And, yes, this is how I learned some of the principles of OOD, long before I knew what an object was.

The benefits were enormous. Not only could we deploy individual chips, we could also make patches in the field by moving functions into RAM and rerouting the vectors. This made field debugging and hot patching much easier.

But I digress. When Ken came to me and asked me to fix this problem he suggested something about pointers to functions. I spent a day or two formalizing the idea and then presented him with a detailed plan. He asked me how long it would take, and I responded that it would take me about a month.

It took *three* months.

I've only been drunk two times in my life, and only *really* drunk once. It was at the Teradyne Christmas party in 1978. I was 26 years old.

The party was held at the Teradyne office, which was mostly open lab space. Everybody got there early, and then there was a huge blizzard that prevented the band and the caterer from getting there. Fortunately there was plenty of booze.

I don't remember much of that night. And what I *do* remember I wish I didn't. But I will share one poignant moment with you.

I was sitting cross-legged on the floor with Ken (my boss, who was all of 29 years old at the time and *not* drunk) weeping about how long the vectorization job was taking me. The alcohol had released my pent up fears and insecurities about my estimate. I don't *think* my head was in his lap, but my memory just isn't very clear about that kind of detail.

I do remember asking him if he was mad at me, and if he thought it was taking me too long. Although the night was a blur, his response has remained clear through the following decades. He said, "Yes, I think it's taken you a long time, but I can see that you are working hard on it, and making good progress. It's something we really need. So, no, I'm not mad."

WHAT IS AN ESTIMATE?

The problem is that we view estimates in different ways. Business likes to view estimates as commitments. Developers like to view estimates as guesses. The difference is profound.

A COMMITMENT

A commitment is something you must achieve. If you commit to getting something done by a certain date, then you simply *have* to get it done by that date. If that means you have to work 12 hours a day, on weekends, skipping family vacations, then so be it. You've made the commitment, and you have to honor it.

Professionals don't make commitments unless they *know* they can achieve them. It's really as simple as that. If you are asked to commit to something that you aren't *certain* you can do, then you are honor bound to decline. If you are asked to commit to a date that you know you *can* achieve, but would require long hours, weekends, and skipped family vacations, then the choice is yours; but you'd better be willing to do what it takes.

Commitment is about *certainty*. Other people are going to accept your commitments and make plans based upon them. The cost of missing those commitments, to them, and to your reputation, is enormous. Missing a commitment is an act of dishonesty only slightly less onerous than an overt lie.

AN ESTIMATE

An estimate is a guess. No commitment is implied. No promise is made. Missing an estimate is not in any way dishonorable. The reason we make estimates is because *we don't know* how long something will take.

Unfortunately, most software developers are terrible estimators. This is not because there's some secret skill to estimating—there's not. The reason we are often so bad at estimating is because we don't understand the true nature of an estimate.

An estimate is not a number. An estimate is a *distribution*. Consider:

Mike: "What is your estimate for completing the Frazzle task?"
Peter: "Three days."

Is Peter really going to be done in three days? It's possible, but how likely is it? The answer to that is: We have no idea. What did Peter mean, and what has Mike learned? If Mike comes back in three days, should he be surprised if Peter is not done? Why would he be? Peter has not made a commitment. Peter has not told him how likely three days is versus four days or five days.

What would have happened if Mike had asked Peter how likely his estimate of three days was?

Mike: "How likely is it that you'll be done in three days?
Peter: "Pretty likely."
Mike: "Can you put a number on it?"
Peter: "Fifty or sixty percent."
Mike: "So there's a good chance that it'll take you four days."
Peter: "Yes, in fact it might even take me five or six, though I doubt it."
Mike: "How much do you doubt it?"
Peter: "Oh, I don't know … I'm ninety-five percent certain I'll be done before six days have passed."
Mike: "You mean it might be seven days?"
Peter: "Well, only if everything goes wrong. Heck, if *everything* goes wrong, it could take me ten or even eleven days. But it's not very likely that so much will go wrong."

Now we're starting to hone in on the truth. Peter's estimate is a *probability distribution*. In his mind, Peter sees the likelihood of completion like what is shown is Figure 10-1.

You can see why Peter gave the original estimate as three days. It's the highest bar on the chart. So in Peter's mind it is the most likely duration for the task. But Mike sees things differently. He looks at the right-hand tail of the chart and worries that Peter might really take eleven days to finish.

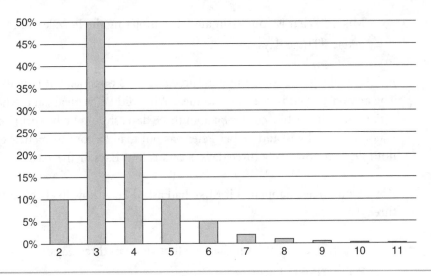

Figure 10-1 Probability distribution

Should Mike be worried about this? Of course! Murphy[1] will have his way with Peter, so some things are probably going to go wrong.

IMPLIED COMMITMENTS

So now Mike has a problem. He's uncertain about the time it will take Peter to get the task done. To minimize that uncertainty he may ask Peter for a commitment. This is something the Peter is in no position to give.

> Mike: "Peter, can you give me a hard date when you'll be done?"
>
> Peter: "No, Mike. Like I said, it'll probably be done in three, maybe four, days."
>
> Mike: "Can we say four then?"
>
> Peter: "No, it *could* be five or six."

So far, everyone is behaving fairly. Mike has asked for a commitment and Peter has carefully declined to give him one. So Mike tries a different tack:

---

1. Murphy's Law holds that if anything can go wrong, it will go wrong.

Mike: "OK, Peter, but can you *try* to make it no more than six days?"

Mike's plea sounds innocent enough, and Mike certainly has no ill intentions. But what, exactly, is Mike asking Peter to do? What does it mean to "try"?

We talked about this before, back in Chapter 2. The word *try* is a loaded term. If Peter agrees to "try" then he is committing to six days. There's no other way to interpret it. Agreeing to try is agreeing to succeed.

What other interpretation could there be? What is it, precisely, that Peter is going to do in order to "try"? Is he going to work more than eight hours? That's clearly implied. Is he going to work weekends? Yes, that's implied too. Will he skip family vacations? Yes, that also part of the implication. All of those things are part of "trying." If Peter doesn't do those things, then Mike could accuse him of not trying hard enough.

Professionals draw a clear distinction between estimates and commitments. They do not commit unless they know for certain they will succeed. They are careful not to make any *implied* commitments. They communicate the probability distribution of their estimates as clearly as possible, so that managers can make appropriate plans.

PERT

In 1957, the Program Evaluation and Review Technique (PERT) was created to support the U.S. Navy's Polaris submarine project. One of the elements of PERT is the way that estimates are calculated. The scheme provides a very simple, but very effective way to convert estimates into probability distributions suitable for managers.

When you estimate a task, you provide three numbers. This is called *trivariate analysis*:

- **O**: Optimistic Estimate. This number is *wildly* optimistic. You could only get the task done this quickly if absolutely everything went right. Indeed, in order for the math to work this number should have much less than a

1% chance of occurrence.[2] In Peter's case, this would be 1 day, as shown in Figure 10-1.

- **N**: Nominal Estimate. This is the estimate with the greatest chance of success. If you were to draw a bar chart, it would be the highest bar, as shown in Figure 10-1. It is 3 days.

- **P**: Pessimistic Estimate. Once again this is *wildly* pessimistic. It should include everything except hurricanes, nuclear war, stray black holes, and other catastrophes. Again, the math only works if this number has much less than a 1% chance of success. In Peter's case this number is off the chart on the right. So 12 days.

Given these three estimates, we can describe the probability distribution as follows:

- $$\mu = \frac{O + 4N + P}{6}$$

μ is the expected duration of the task. In Peter's case it is $(1+12+12)/6$, or about 4.2 days. For most tasks this will be a somewhat pessimistic number because the right-hand tail of the distribution is longer than the left-hand tail.[3]

- $$\sigma = \frac{P - O}{6}$$

σ is the standard deviation[4] of the probability distribution for the task. It is a measure of how uncertain the task is. When this number is large, the uncertainty is large too. For Peter this number is $(12 - 1)/6$, or about 1.8 days.

Given Peter's estimate of 4.2/1.8, Mike understands that this task will likely be done within five days but might also take 6, or even 9, days to complete.

---

2. The precise number for a normal distribution is 1:769, or 0.13%, or 3 sigma. Odds of one in a thousand are probably safe.

3. PERT presumes that this approximates a beta distribution. This makes sense since the minimum duration for a task is often much more certain than the maximum. [McConnell2006] Fig. 1-3.

4. If you don't know what a standard deviation is, you should find a good summary of probability and statistics. The concept is not hard to understand, and it will serve you very well.

But Mike is not just managing one task. He's managing a project of many tasks. Peter has three of those tasks that he must work on in sequence. Peter has estimated these tasks as shown in Table 10-1.

Table 10-1 Peter's Tasks

Task	Optimistic	Nominal	Pessimistic	μ	σ
Alpha	1	3	12	4.2	1.8
Beta	1	1.5	14	3.5	2.2
Gamma	3	6.25	11	6.5	1.3

What's up with that "beta" task? It looks like Peter is pretty confident about it, but that something could possibly go wrong that would derail him significantly. How should Mike interpret that? How long should Mike plan for Peter to complete all three tasks?

It turns out that, with a few simple calculations, Mike can combine all of Peter's tasks and come up with a probability distribution for the entire set of tasks. The math is pretty straightforward:

- $\mu_{sequence} = \sum \mu_{task}$

  For any sequence of tasks the expected duration of that sequence is the simple sum of all the expected durations of the tasks in that sequence. So if Peter has three tasks to complete, and their estimates are 4.2/1.8, 3.5/2.2, and 6.5/1.3, then Peter will likely be done with all three in about 14 days: 4.2 + 3.5 + 6.5.

- $\sigma_{sequence} = \sqrt{\sum \sigma_{task}^2}$

  The standard deviation of the sequence is the square root of the sum of the squares of the standard deviations of the tasks. So the standard deviation for all three of Peter's tasks is about 3.

$$(1.8^2 + 2.2^2 + 1.3^2)^{1/2} =$$
$$(3.24 + 2.48 + 1.69)^{1/2} =$$
$$9.77^{1/2} = \sim 3.13$$

This tells Mike that Peter's tasks will likely take 14 days, but could very well take 17 days (1σ) and could possibly even take 20 days (2σ). It could even take longer, but that's pretty unlikely.

Look back at the table of estimates. Can you feel the pressure to get all three tasks done in five days? After all, the best-case estimates are 1, 1, and 3. Even the nominal estimates only add up to 10 days. How did we get all the way up to 14 days, with a possibility of 17 or 20? The answer is that the uncertainty in those tasks compounds in a way that adds *realism* to the plan.

If you are a programmer of more than a few years' experience, you've likely seen projects that were estimated optimistically, and that took three to five times longer than hoped. The simple PERT scheme just shown is one reasonable way to help prevent setting optimistic expectations. Software professionals are very careful to set reasonable expectations despite the pressure to *try* to go fast.

ESTIMATING TASKS

Mike and Peter were making a terrible mistake. Mike was asking Peter how long his tasks would take. Peter gave honest trivariate answers, but what about the opinions of his teammates? Might they have a different idea?

The most important estimation resource you have are the people around you. They can see things that you don't. They can help you estimate your tasks more accurately than you can estimate them on your own.

WIDEBAND DELPHI

In the 1970s Barry Boehm introduced us to an estimation technique called "wideband delphi."[5] There have been many variations over the years. Some are formal, some are informal; but they all have one thing in common: consensus.

The strategy is simple. A team of people assemble, discuss a task, estimate the task, and iterate the discussion and estimation until they reach agreement.

---

5. [Boehm81]

The original approach outlined by Boehm involved several meetings and documents that involve too much ceremony and overhead for my tastes. I prefer simple low-overhead approaches such as the following.

Flying Fingers

Everybody sits around a table. Tasks are discussed one at a time. For each task there is discussion about what the task involves, what might confound or complicate it, and how it might be implemented. Then the participants put their hands below the table and raise 0 to 5 fingers based on how long they think the task will take. The moderator counts 1-2-3, and all the participants show their hands at once.

If everyone agrees, then they go on to the next task. Otherwise they continue the discussion to determine why they disagree. They repeat this until they agree.

Agreement does not need to be absolute. As long as the estimates are close, it's good enough. So, for example, a smattering of 3s and 4s is agreement. However if everyone holds up 4 fingers except for one person who holds up 1 finger, then they have something to talk about.

The scale of the estimate is decided on at the beginning of the meeting. It might be the number of days for a task, or it might be some more interesting scale such as "fingers times three" or "fingers squared."

The simultaneity of displaying the fingers is important. We don't want people changing their estimates based on what they see other people do.

Planning Poker

In 2002 James Grenning wrote a delightful paper[6] describing "Planning Poker." This variation of wideband delphi has become so popular that several different companies have used the idea to make marketing giveaways in the form of planning poker card decks.[7] There is even a web site named planningpoker.com that you can use to do planning poker on the Net with distributed teams.

---

6. [Grenning2002]

7. http://store.mountaingoatsoftware.com/products/planning-poker-cards

The idea is very simple. For each member of the estimation team, deal a hand of cards with different numbers on them. The numbers 0 through 5 work fine, and make this system logically equivalent to *flying fingers*.

Pick a task and discuss it. At some point the moderator asks everyone to pick a card. The members of the team pull out a card that matches their estimate and hold it up with the back facing outward so that no one else can see the value of the card. Then the moderator tells everyone to show their cards.

The rest is just like flying fingers. If there is agreement, then the estimate is accepted. Otherwise the cards are returned to the hand, and the players continue to discuss the task.

Much "science" has been dedicated to choosing the correct card values for a hand. Some folks have gone so far as to use cards based on a Fibonacci series. Others have included cards for infinity and question mark. Personally, I think five cards labeled 0, 1, 3, 5, 10 are sufficient.

Affinity Estimation

A particularly unique variation of wideband delphi was shown to me several years ago by Lowell Lindstrom. I've had quite a bit of good luck with this approach with various customers and teams.

All the tasks are written onto cards, without any estimates showing. The estimation team stands around a table or a wall with the cards spread out randomly. The team members do not talk, they simply start sorting the cards relative to one another. Tasks that take longer are moved to the right. Smaller tasks move to the left.

Any team member can move any card at any time, even if it has already been moved by another member. Any card moved more than η times is set aside for discussion.

Eventually the silent sorting peters out and discussion can begin. Disagreements about the ordering of the cards are explored. There may be some quick design sessions or some quick hand-drawn wire frames to help gain consensus.

The next step is to draw lines between the cards that represent bucket sizes. These buckets might be in days, weeks, or points. Five buckets in a Fibonacci sequence (1, 2, 3, 5, 8) is traditional.

Trivariate Estimates

These wideband delphi techniques are good for choosing a single nominal estimate for a task. But as we stated earlier, most of the time we want three estimates so that we can create a probability distribution. The optimistic and pessimistic values for each task can be generated very quickly using any of the wideband delphi variants. For example, if you are using planning poker, you simply ask the team to hold up the cards for their pessimistic estimate and then take the highest. You do the same for the optimistic estimate and take the lowest.

THE LAW OF LARGE NUMBERS

Estimates are fraught with error. That's why they are called estimates. One way of managing error is to take advantage of the *Law of Large Numbers*.[8] An implication of this law is that if you break up a large task into many smaller tasks and estimate them independently, the sum of the estimates of the small tasks will be more accurate than a single estimate of the larger task. The reason for this increase in accuracy is that the errors in the small tasks tend to integrate out.

Frankly, this is optimistic. Errors in estimates tend toward underestimation and not overestimation, so the integration is hardly perfect. That being said, breaking large tasks into small ones and estimating the small ones independently is still a good technique. Some of the errors *do* integrate out, and breaking the tasks up is a good way to understand those tasks better and uncover surprises.

CONCLUSION

Professional software developers know how to provide the business with practical estimates that the business can use for planning purposes. They do not make promises that they can't keep, and they don't make commitments that they aren't sure they can meet.

---

8. http://en.wikipedia.org/wiki/Law_of_large_numbers

When professionals make commitments, they provide *hard* numbers, and then they make those numbers. However, in most cases professionals do not make such committments. Rather, they provide probabilistic estimates that describe the expected completion time and the likely variance.

Professional developers work with the other members of their team to achieve consensus on the estimates that are given to management.

The techniques described in this chapter are *examples* of some of the different ways that professional developers create practical estimates. These are not the only such techniques and are not necessarily the best. They are simply techniques that I have found to work well for me.

BIBLIOGRAPHY

[**McConnell2006**]: Steve McConnell, *Software Estimation: Demystifying the Black Art*, Redmond, WA: Microsoft Press, 2006.

[**Boehm81**]: Barry W. Boehm, *Software Engineering Economics*, Upper Saddle River, NJ: Prentice Hall, 1981.

[**Grenning2002**]: James Grenning, "Planning Poker or How to Avoid Analysis Paralysis while Release Planning," April 2002, http://renaissancesoftware. net/papers/14-papers/44-planing-poker.html

PRESSURE
11

Imagine that you are having an out-of-body experience, observing yourself on an operating table while a surgeon performs open heart surgery on you. That surgeon is trying to save your life, but time is limited so he is operating under a deadline—a *literal* deadline.

How do you want that doctor to behave? Do you want him to appear calm and collected? Do you want him issuing clear and precise orders to his support staff? Do you want him following his training and adhering to his disciplines?

Or do you want him sweating and swearing? Do you want him slamming and throwing instruments? Do you want him blaming management for unrealistic expectations and continuously complaining about the time? Do you want him behaving like a professional, or like a typical developer?

The professional developer is calm and decisive under pressure. As the pressure grows he adheres to his training and disciplines, knowing that they are the best way to meet the deadlines and commitments that are pressing on him.

In 1988 I was working at Clear Communications. This was a start-up that never quite got started. We burned through our first round of financing and then had to go for a second, and then a third.

The initial product vision sounded good, but the product architecture could never seem to get grounded. At first the product was both software and hardware. Then it became software only. The software platform changed from PCs to Sparcstations. The customers changed from high end to low end. Eventually, even the original intent of the product drifted as the company tried to find something that would generate revenue. In the nearly four years I spent there, I don't think the company saw a penny of income.

Needless to say, we software developers were under significant pressure. There were quite a few very long nights, and even longer weekends spent in the office at the terminal. Functions were written in C that were *3,000 lines long*. There were arguments with shouting and name calling. There was intrigue and subterfuge. There were fists punched through walls, pens thrown angrily at whiteboards, caricatures of annoying colleagues embossed into walls with the tips of pencils, and there was a never ending supply of anger and stress.

Deadlines were driven by events. Features had to be made ready for trade shows or customer demos. Anything a customer asked for, regardless of how silly, we'd have ready for the next demo. Time was always too short. Work was always behind. Schedules were always overwhelming.

If you worked 80 hours in a week, you could be a hero. If you hacked some mess together for a customer demo, you could be a hero. If you did it enough, you could be promoted. If you didn't, you could be fired. It was a start-up—it was all about the "sweat equity." And in 1988, with nearly 20 years' experience under my belt, I bought into it.

I was the development manager telling the programmers who worked for me that they had to work more and faster. I was one of the 80-hour guys, writing 3,000-line C functions at 2 AM while my children slept at home without their father in the house. I was the one who threw the pens and shouted. I got people fired if they didn't shape up. It was awful. I was awful.

Then came the day when my wife forced me to take a good long look in the mirror. I didn't like what I saw. She told me I just wasn't very nice to be around. I had to agree. But I didn't like it, so I stormed out of the house in anger and started walking without a destination. I walked for thirty minutes or so, seething as I strode; and then it started to rain.

And something clicked inside my head. I started to laugh. I laughed at my folly. I laughed at my stress. I laughed at the man in the mirror, the poor schmuck who'd been making life miserable for himself and others in the name of—what?

Everything changed that day. I stopped the crazy hours. I stopped the high-stress lifestyle. I stopped throwing pens and writing 3,000-line C functions. I determined that I was going to enjoy my career by doing it well, not by doing it stupidly.

I left that job as professionally as I could, and I became a consultant. Since that day I've never called another person "boss."

AVOIDING PRESSURE

The best way to stay calm under pressure is to avoid the situations that *cause* pressure. That avoidance may not eliminate the pressure completely, but it can go a long way towards minimizing and shortening the high-pressure periods.

COMMITMENTS

As we discovered in Chapter 10, it is important to avoid committing to deadlines that we aren't sure we can meet. The business will always want these commitments because they want to eliminate risk. What we must do is make sure that the risk is quantified and presented to the business so that they can manage it appropriately. Accepting unrealistic commitments thwarts this goal and does a disservice to both the business and to ourselves.

Sometimes commitments are made for us. Sometimes we find that our business has made promises to the customers without consulting us. When this happens we are honor bound to help the business find a way to meet those commitments. However, we are *not* honor bound to *accept* the commitments.

The difference is important. Professionals will always help the business find a way to achieve its goals. But professionals do not necessarily accept commitments made for them by the business. In the end, if we can find no way to meet the promises made by the business, then the people who made the promises must accept the responsibility.

This is easy to say. But when your business is failing, and your paycheck is delayed because of missed commitments, it's hard not to feel the pressure. But if you have behaved professionally, at least you can hold your head high as you hunt for a new job.

STAYING CLEAN

The way to go fast, and to keep the deadlines at bay, is to stay clean. Professionals do not succumb to the temptation to create a mess in order to move quickly. Professionals realize that "quick and dirty" is an oxymoron. Dirty always means slow!

We can avoid pressure by keeping our systems, our code, and our design as clean as possible. This does not mean that we spend endless hours polishing code. It simply means that we don't tolerate messes. We know that messes will slow us down, causing us to miss dates and break commitments. So we do the best work we can and keep our output as clean as we can.

CRISIS DISCIPLINE

You know what you believe by observing yourself in a crisis. If in a crisis you follow your disciplines, then you truly believe in those disciplines. On the other hand, if you change your behavior in a crisis, then you don't truly believe in your normal behavior.

If you follow the discipline of Test Driven Development in noncrisis times but abandon it during a crisis, then you don't really trust that TDD is helpful. If you keep your code clean during normal times but make messes in a crisis, then you don't really believe that messes slow you down. If you pair in a crisis but don't normally pair, then you believe pairing is more efficient than non-pairing.

Choose disciplines that you feel comfortable following in a crisis. *Then follow them all the time.* Following these disciplines is the best way to avoid getting into a crisis.

Don't change your behavior when the crunch comes. If your disciplines are the best way to work, then they should be followed even in the depths of a crisis.

HANDLING PRESSURE

Forestalling, mitigating, and eliminating pressure is all well and good, but sometimes the pressure comes despite all your best intentions and preventions. Sometimes the project just takes longer than anyone thought it would. Sometimes the initial design is just wrong and must be reworked. Sometimes you lose a valued team member or customer. Sometimes you make a commitment that you just can't keep. Then what?

DON'T PANIC

Manage your stress. Sleepless nights won't help you get done any faster. Sitting and fretting won't help either. And the worst thing you could do is to rush! Resist that temptation at all costs. Rushing will only drive you deeper into the hole.

Instead, slow down. Think the problem through. Plot a course to the best possible outcome, and then drive towards that outcome at a reasonable and steady pace.

COMMUNICATE

Let your team and your superiors know that you are in trouble. Tell them your best plans for getting out of trouble. Ask them for their input and guidance. Avoid creating surprises. Nothing makes people more angry and less rational than surprises. Surprises multiply the pressure by ten.

RELY ON YOUR DISCIPLINES

When the going gets tough, *trust your disciplines.* The reason you *have* disciplines is to give you guidance through times of high pressure. These are the times to pay special attention to all your disciplines. These are *not* the times to question or abandon them.

Instead of looking around in a panic for something, anything, that will help you get done faster, become more deliberate and dedicated to following your chosen disciplines. If you follow TDD, then write even more tests than usual. If you are a merciless refactorer, then refactor even more. If you keep your functions small, then keep them even smaller. The only way through the pressure cooker is to rely on what you already know works—your disciplines.

GET HELP

Pair! When the heat is on, find an associate who is willing to pair program with you. You will get done faster, with fewer defects. Your pair partner will help you hold on to your disciplines and keep you from panicking. Your partner will spot things that you miss, will have helpful ideas, and will pick up the slack when you lose focus.

By the same token, when you see someone else who's under pressure, offer to pair with them. Help them out of the hole they are in.

CONCLUSION

The trick to handling pressure is to avoid it when you can, and weather it when you can't. You avoid it by managing commitments, following your disciplines, and keeping clean. You weather it by staying calm, communicating, following your disciplines, and getting help.

Collaboration

Most software is created by teams. Teams are most effective when the team members collaborate professionally. It is unprofessional to be a loner or a recluse on a team.

In 1974 I was 22. My marriage to my wonderful wife, Ann Marie, was barely six months old. The birth of my first child, Angela, was still a year away. And I worked at a division of Teradyne known as Chicago Laser Systems.

Working next to me was my high school buddy, Tim Conrad. Tim and I had worked quite a few miracles in our time. We built computers together in his basement. We built Jacob's ladders in mine. We taught each other how to program PDP-8s and how to wire up integrated circuits and transistors into functioning calculators.

We were programmers working on a system that used lasers to trim electronic components like resistors and capacitors to extremely high accuracy. For example, we trimmed the crystal for the first digital watch, the Motorola Pulsar.

The computer we programmed was the M365, Teradyne's PDP-8 clone. We wrote in assembly language, and our source files were kept on magnetic tape cartridges. Although we could edit on a screen, the process was quite involved, so we used printed listings for most of our code reading and preliminary editing.

We had no facility at all for searching the code base. There was no way to find out all the places where a given function was called or a given constant was used. As you might imagine, this was quite a hindrance.

So one day Tim and I decided we would write a cross-reference generator. This program would read in our source tapes and print out a listing of every symbol, along with the file and line numbers where that symbol was used.

The initial program was pretty simple to write. It simply read in the source tape, parsed the assembler syntax, created a symbol table, and added references to the entries. It worked great, but it was horribly slow. It took over an hour to process our Master Operating Program (the MOP).

The reason it was so slow was that we were holding the growing symbol table in a single memory buffer. Whenever we found a new reference we inserted it into the buffer, moving the rest of the buffer down by a few bytes to make room.

Tim and I were not experts on data structures and algorithms. We'd never heard of hash tables or binary searches. We had no clue how to make an algorithm fast. We just knew that what we were doing was too slow.

So we tried one thing after another. We tried putting the references in linked lists. We tried leaving gaps in the array and only growing the buffer when the gaps filled. We tried creating linked lists of gaps. We tried all kinds of crazy ideas.

We stood at the whiteboard in our office and drew diagrams of our data structures and performed calculations to predict performance. We'd get to the office every day with another new idea. We collaborated like fiends.

Some of the things we tried increased performance. Some slowed it down. It was maddening. This was when I first discovered how hard it is to optimize software, and how nonintuitive the process is.

In the end we got the time down under 15 minutes, which was very close to how long it took simply to read the source tape. So we were satisfied.

PROGRAMMERS VERSUS PEOPLE

We didn't become programmers because we like working with people. As a rule we find interpersonal relationships messy and unpredictable. We like the clean and predictable behavior of the machines that we program. We are happiest when we are alone in a room for hours deeply focussing on some really interesting problem.

OK, that's a huge overgeneralization and there are loads of exceptions. There are plenty of programmers who are good at working with people and enjoy the challenge. But the group average still tends in the direction I stated. We, programmers, enjoy the mild sensory deprivation and cocoonlike immersion of *focus*.

PROGRAMMERS VERSUS EMPLOYERS

In the seventies and eighties, while working as a programmer at Teradyne, I learned to be *really* good at debugging. I loved the challenge and would throw myself at problems with vigor and enthusiasm. No bug could hide long from me!

When I solved a bug it was like winning a victory, or slaying the Jabberwock! I would go to my boss, Ken Finder, Vorpal blade in hand, and passionately describe to him how *interesting* the bug was. One day Ken finally erupted in frustration: "Bugs aren't interesting. Bugs just need to be fixed!"

I learned something that day. It's good to be passionate about what we do. But it's also good to keep your eye on the goals of the people who pay you.

The first responsibility of the professional programmer is to meet the needs of his or her employer. That means collaborating with your managers, business analysts, testers, and other team members to *deeply understand* the business goals. This doesn't mean you have to become a business wonk. It *does* mean that you need to understand why you are writing the code you are writing, and how the business that employs you will benefit from it.

The worst thing a professional programmer can do is to blissfully bury himself in a tomb of technology while the business crashes and burns around him. Your *job* is to keep the business afloat!

So, professional programmers take the time to understand the business. They talk to users about the software they are using. They talk to sales and marketing people about the problems and issues they have. They talk to their managers to understand the short- and long-term goals of the team.

In short, they pay attention to the ship they are sailing on.

The only time I was fired from a programming job was in 1976. I was working for Outboard Marine Corp. at the time. I was helping to write a factory automation system that used IBM System/7s to monitor dozens of aluminum die-cast machines on the shop floor.

Technically, this was a challenging and rewarding job. The architecture of the System/7 was fascinating, and the factory automation system itself was really interesting.

We also had a good team. The team lead, John, was competent and motivated. My two programming teammates were pleasant and helpful. We had a lab dedicated to our project, and we all worked in that lab. The business partner was engaged and in the lab with us. Our manager, Ralph, was competent, focused, and in charge.

Everything should have been great. The problem was me. I was enthusiastic enough about the project, and about the technology, but at the grand old age of 24 I simply could not bring myself to care about the business or about its internal political structure.

My first mistake was on my first day. I showed up without wearing a tie. I had worn one on my interview, and I had seen that everyone else wore ties, but I failed to make the connection. So on my first day, Ralph came to me and plainly said, "We wear ties here."

I can't tell you how much I resented that. It bothered me at a deep level. I wore the tie everyday, and I hated it. But why? I knew what I was getting into. I knew the conventions they had adopted. Why would I be so upset? Because I was a selfish, narcissistic little twerp.

I simply could not get to work on time. And I thought it didn't matter. After all, I was doing "a good job." And it was true, I was doing a very good job at writing my programs. I was easily the best technical programmer on the team. I could write code faster and better than the others. I could diagnose and solve problems quicker. I *knew* I was valuable. So times and dates didn't matter much to me.

The decision to fire me was made one day when I failed to show on time for a milestone. Apparently John had told us all that he wanted a demo of working features next Monday. I'm sure I knew about this, but dates and times simply weren't important to me.

We were in active development. The system was not in production. There was no reason to leave the system running when no one was in the lab. I must have been the last one to leave that Friday, and apparently I left the system in a nonfunctioning state. The fact that Monday was important had simply not stuck in my brain.

I came in an hour late that Monday and saw everyone gathered glumly around a nonfunctioning system. John asked me, "Why isn't the system working today, Bob?" My answer: "I don't know." And I sat down to debug it. I was still clueless about the Monday demo, but I could tell by everyone else's body language that something was wrong. Then John came over and whispered in my ear, "What if Stenberg had decided to visit?" Then he walked away in disgust.

Stenberg was the VP in charge of automation. Nowadays we'd call him a CIO. The question held no meaning for me. "So what?" I thought. "The system isn't in production, what's the big deal?"

I got my first warning letter later that day. It told me I had to change my attitude immediately or "quick termination will be the result." I was horrified!

I took some time to analyze my behavior and began to realize what I had been doing wrong. I talked with John and Ralph about it. I determined to turn myself and my job around.

And I did! I stopped coming in late. I started paying attention to internal politics. I began to understand why John was worried about Stenberg. I began to see the bad situation I had put him in by not having that system running on Monday.

But it was too little, too late. The die was cast. I got a second warning letter a month later for a trivial error that I made. I should have realized at that point that the letters were a formality and that the decision to terminate me had already been made. But I was determined to rescue the situation. So I worked even harder.

The termination meeting came a few weeks later.

I went home that day to my pregnant 22-year-old wife and had to tell her that I'd been fired. That's not an experience I ever want to repeat.

PROGRAMMERS VERSUS PROGRAMMERS

Programmers often have difficulty working closely with other programmers. This leads to some really terrible problems.

Owned Code

One of the worst symptoms of a dysfunctional team is when each programmer builds a wall around *his* code and refuses to let other programmers touch it. I have been to places where the programmers wouldn't even let other programmers *see* their code. This is a recipe for disaster.

I once consulted for a company that built high-end printers. These machines have many different components such as feeders, printers, stackers, staplers, cutters, and so on. The business valued each of these devices differently. Feeders were more important than stackers, and nothing was more important than the printer.

Each programmer worked on *his* device. One guy would write the code for the feeder, another guy would write the code for the stapler. Each of them kept their technology to themselves and prevented anyone else from touching their code. The political clout that these programmers wielded was directly related to how much the business valued the device. The programmer who worked on the printer was unassailable.

This was a disaster for the technology. As a consultant I was able to see that there was massive duplication in the code and that the interfaces between the modules were completely skewed. But no amount of argument on my part could convince the programmers (or the business) to change their ways. After all, their salary reviews were tied to the importance of the devices they maintained.

Collective Ownership

It is far better to break down all walls of code ownership and have the team own all the code. I prefer teams in which any team member can check out any module and make any changes they think are appropriate. I want the *team* to own the code, not the individuals.

Professional developers do not prevent others from working in the code. They do not build walls of ownership around code. Rather, they work with each other on as much of the system as they can. They learn from each other by working with each other on other parts of the system.

Pairing

Many programmers dislike the idea of pair-programming. I find this odd since most programmers *will* pair in emergencies. Why? Because it is clearly the most efficient way to solve the problem. It just goes back to the old adage: Two heads are better than one. But if pairing is the most efficient way to solve a problem in an emergency, why isn't it the most efficient way to solve a problem period?

I'm not going to quote studies at you, although there are some that could be quoted. I'm not going to tell you any anecdotes, although there are many I could tell. I'm not even going to tell you how much you should pair. All I'm going to tell you is that *professionals pair*. Why? Because for at least some problems it is the most efficient way to solve them. But that's not the only reason.

Professionals also pair because it is the best way to share knowledge with each other. Professionals don't create knowledge silos. Rather, they learn the different parts of the system and business by pairing with each other. They recognize that although all team members have a position to play, all team members should also be able play another position in a pinch.

Professionals pair because it is the best way to review code. No system should consist of code that hasn't been reviewed by other programmers. There are many ways to conduct code reviews; most of them are horrifically inefficient. The most efficient and effective way to review code is to collaborate in writing it.

CEREBELLUMS

I rode the train into Chicago one morning in 2000 during the height of the dot com boom. As I stepped off the train onto the platform I was assaulted by a huge billboard hanging above the exit doors. The sign was for a well-known software firm that was recruiting programmers. It read: *Come rub cerebellums with the best.*

I was immediately struck by the rank stupidity of a sign like that. These poor clueless advertising people were trying to appeal to a highly technical, intelligent, and knowledgeable population of programmers. These are the kind of people who don't suffer stupidity particularly well. The advertisers were trying to evoke the image of knowledge sharing with other highly intelligent people. Unfortunately they referred to a part of the brain, the cerebellum, that deals with fine muscle control, not intelligence. So the very people they were trying to attract were sneering at such a silly error.

But something else intrigued me about that sign. It made me think of a group of people trying to rub cerebellums. Since the cerebellum is at the back of the brain, the best way to rub cerebellums is to face away from each other. I imagined a team of programmers in cubicles, sitting in corners with their backs to each other, staring at screens while wearing headphones. *That's* how you rub cerebellums. That's also not a team.

Professionals work *together*. You can't work together while you are sitting in corners wearing headphones. So I want you sitting around tables *facing* each other. I want you to be able to smell each other's fear. I want you to be able to overhear someone's frustrated mutterings. I want serendipitous communication, both verbal and body language. I want you communicating as a unit.

Perhaps you believe that you work better when you work alone. That may be true, but it doesn't mean that the *team* works better when you work alone. And, in fact, it's highly unlikely that you *do* work better when you work alone.

There are times when working alone is the right thing to do. There are times when you simply need to think long and hard about a problem. There are times when the task is so trivial that it would be a waste to have another person working with you. But, in general, it is best to collaborate closely with others and to pair with them a large fraction of the time.

CONCLUSION

Perhaps we didn't get into programming to work with people. Tough luck for us. Programming *is all about working with people.* We need to work with our business, and we need to work with each other.

I know, I know. Wouldn't it be great if they just shut us into a room with six massive screens, a T3 pipe, a parallel array of superfast processors, unlimited ram and disk, and a never-ending supply of diet cola and spicy corn chips? Alas, it is not to be. If we really want to spend our days programming, we are going to have to learn to talk to—people.[1]

---

1. A reference to the last word in the movie *Soylent Green.*

TEAMS AND PROJECTS 13

What if you have lots of little projects to get done? How should you allocate those projects to the programmers? What if you have one really huge project to get done?

DOES IT BLEND?

I have consulted for a number of banks and insurance companies over the years. One thing they seem to have in common is the odd way they partition projects.

Often a project at a bank will be a relatively small job that requires one or two programmers for a few weeks. This project will often be staffed with a project manager, who is also managing other projects. It will be staffed with a business analyst, who is also providing requirements for other projects. It will be staffed with some programmers who are also working on other projects. A tester or two will be assigned, and they too will be working on other projects.

See the pattern? The project is so small that no individual can be assigned to it on a full-time basis. Everybody is working on the project at 50, or even 25, percent.

Now here's a rule: There is no such thing as half a person.

It makes no sense to tell a programer to devote half their time to project A and the rest of their time to project B, especially when the two projects have two different project managers, different business analysts, different programmers, and different testers. How in Hell's kitchen can you call a monstrosity like that a team? That's not a team, that's something that came out of a Waring blender.

THE GELLED TEAM

It take time for a team to form. The team members start to form relationships. They learn how to collaborate with each other. They learn each other's quirks, strengths, and weaknesses. Eventually the team begins to *gel*.

There is something truly magical about a gelled team. They can work miracles. They anticipate each other, cover for each other, support each other, and demand the best from each other. They make things happen.

A gelled team usually consists of about a dozen people. It could be as many as twenty or as few as three, but the best number is probably around twelve. The team should be composed of programmers, testers, and analysts. And it should have a project manager.

The ratio of programmers to testers and analysts can vary greatly, but 2:1 is a good number. So a nicely gelled team of twelve might have seven programmers, two testers, two analysts, and a project manager.

The analysts develop the requirements and write automated acceptance tests for them. The testers also write automated acceptance tests. The difference between the two is perspective. Both are writing requirements. But analysts focus on business value; testers focus on correctness. Analysts write the happy path cases; testers worry about what might go wrong, and write the failure and boundary cases.

The project manager tracks the progress of the team, and makes sure the team understands the schedules and priorities.

One of the team members may play a part-time role of coach, or master, with responsibility for defending the team's process and disciplines. They act as the team conscience when the team is tempted to go off-process because of schedule pressure.

Fermentation

It takes time for a team like this to work out their differences, come to terms with each other, and really gel. It might take six months. It might even take a year. But once it happens, it's magic. A gelled team will plan together, solve problems together, face issues together, and *get things done.*

Once this happens, it is ludicrous to break it apart just because a project comes to an end. It's best to keep that team together and just keep feeding it projects.

Which Came First, the Team or the Project?

Banks and insurance companies tried to form teams around projects. This is a foolish approach. The teams simply cannot gel. The individuals are only on the project for a short time, and only for a percentage of their time, and therefore never learn how to deal with each other.

Professional development organizations allocate projects to existing gelled teams, they don't form teams around projects. A gelled team can accept many projects simultaneously and will divvy up the work according to their own opinions, skills, and abilities. The gelled team will get the projects done.

BUT HOW DO YOU MANAGE THAT?

Teams have velocities.[1] The velocity of a team is simply the amount of work it can get done in a fixed period of time. Some teams measure their velocity in *points* per week, where points are a unit of complexity. They break down the features of each project they are working on and estimate them in points. Then they measure how many points they get done per week.

Velocity is a statistical measure. A team might get 38 points done one week, 42 done the next, and 25 done the next. Over time this will average out.

Management can set targets for each project given to a team. For example, if the average velocity of a team is 50 and they have three projects they are working on, then management can ask the team to split their effort into 15, 15, and 20.

Aside from having a gelled team working on your projects, the advantage of this scheme is that in an emergency the business can say, "Project B is in crisis; put 100% of your effort on that project for the next three weeks."

Reallocating priorities that quickly is virtually impossible with the teams that came out of the blender, but gelled teams that are working on two or three projects concurrently can turn on a dime.

THE PROJECT OWNER DILEMMA

One of the objections to the approach I'm advocating is that the project owners lose some security and power. Project owners who have a team dedicated to

---

1. [RCM2003] pp. 20–22; [COHN2006] Look in the index for many excellent references to velocity.

their project can count on the effort of that team. They know that because forming and disbanding a team is an expensive operation, the business will not take the team away for short-term reasons.

On the other hand, if projects are given to gelled teams, and if those teams take on several projects at the same time, then the business is free to change priorities on a whim. This can make the project owner insecure about the future. The resources that project owner is depending on might be suddenly removed from him.

Frankly, I prefer the latter situation. The business should not have its hands tied by the artificial difficulty of forming and disbanding teams. If the business decides that one project is higher priority than another, it should be able to reallocate resources quickly. It is the project owner's responsibility to make the case for his project.

CONCLUSION

Teams are harder to build than projects. Therefore, it is better to form persistent teams that move together from one project to the next and can take on more than one project at a time. The goal in forming a team is to give that team enough time to gel, and then keep it together as an engine for getting many projects done.

BIBLIOGRAPHY

[**RCM2003**]: Robert C. Martin, *Agile Software Development: Principles, Patterns, and Practices,* Upper Saddle River, NJ: Prentice Hall, 2003.

[**COHN2006**]: Mike Cohn, *Agile Estimating and Planning,* Upper Saddle River, NJ: Prentice Hall, 2006.

Mentoring, Apprenticeship, and Craftsmanship

I have been consistently disappointed by the quality of CS graduates. It's not that the graduates aren't bright or talented, it's just that they haven't been taught what programming is really all about.

DEGREES OF FAILURE

I once interviewed a young woman who was working on her master's degree in computer science for a major university. She was applying for a summer intern position. I asked her to write some code with me, and she said "I don't really write code."

Please read the previous paragraph again, and then skip over this one to the next.

I asked her what programming courses she had taken in pursuit of her master's degree. She said that she hadn't taken any.

Maybe you'd like to start at the beginning of the chapter just to be sure you haven't fallen into some alternate universe or have just awakened from a bad dream.

At this point you might well be asking yourself how a student in a CS master's program can avoid a programming course. I wondered the same thing at the time. I'm still wondering today.

Of course, that's the most extreme of a series of disappointments I've had while interviewing graduates. Not all CS graduates are disappointing—far from it! However, I've noticed that those who aren't have something in common: Nearly all of them *taught themselves to program* before they entered university and continued to teach themselves despite university.

Now don't get me wrong. I think it is possible to get an excellent education at a university. It's just that I also think it's possible to wiggle yourself through the system and come out with a diploma, and not much else.

And there's another problem. Even the best CS degree programs do not typically prepare the young graduate for what they will find in industry. This is not an indictment of the degree programs so much as it is the reality of nearly all disciplines. What you learn in school and what you find on the job are often very different things.

MENTORING

How do we learn how to program? Let me tell you my story about being mentored.

DIGI-COMP I, MY FIRST COMPUTER

In 1964 my mother gave me a little plastic computer for my twelfth birthday. It was called a Digi-Comp I.[1] It had three plastic flip-flops and six plastic *and*-gates. You could connect the outputs of the flip-flops to the inputs of the *and*-gates. You could also connect the output of the *and*-gates to the inputs of the flip-flops. In short, this allowed you to create a three-bit finite state machine.

The kit came with a manual that gave you several programs to run. You programmed the machine by pushing little tubes (short segments of soda straws) onto little pegs protruding from the flip flops. The manual told you exactly where to put each tube, but not what the tubes *did*. I found this very frustrating!

I stared at the machine for hours and determined how it worked at the lowest level; but I could not, for the life of me, figure out how to make it do what I wanted it to do. The last page in the manual told me to send in a dollar and they would send back a manual telling me how to program the machine.[2]

I sent in my dollar and waited with the impatience of a twelve year old. The day the manual arrived I devoured it. It was a simple treatise on boolean algebra covering basic factoring of boolean equations, associative and distributive laws, and DeMorgan's theorem. The manual showed how to express a problem in terms of a sequence of boolean equations. It also described how to reduce those equations to fit into 6 *and*-gates.

I conceived of my first program. I still remember the name: Mr. Patternson's Computerized Gate. I wrote the equations, reduced them, and mapped them to the tubes and pegs of the machine. *And it worked!*

Writing those three words just now sent chills down my spine. The same chills that coursed down that twelve year old nearly half a century ago. I was hooked. My life would never be the same.

Do you remember the moment your first program worked? Did it change your life or set you on a course you could not turn away from?

---

1. There are many web sites that offer simulators of this stimulating little computer.
2. I still have this manual. It holds a place of honor on one of my bookshelves.

I did not figure it all out for myself. I was *mentored*. Some very kind and very adept people (to whom I owe a huge debt of gratitude) took the time to write a treatise on boolean algebra that was accessible to a twelve year old. They connected the mathematical theory to the pragmatics of the little plastic computer and empowered me to make that computer do what I wanted it to do.

I just pulled down my copy of that fateful manual. I keep it in a zip-lock bag. Nevertheless, the years have taken their toll by yellowing the pages and making them brittle. Still, the power of the words shines out of them. The elegance of their description of boolean algebra consumed three sparse pages. Their step-by-step walk-through of the equations for each of the original programs is still compelling. It was a work of mastery. It was a work that changed at least one young man's life. Yet I doubt I'll never know the names of the authors.

THE ECP-18 IN HIGH SCHOOL

At the age of fifteen, as a freshman in high school, I liked hanging out in the math department. (Go figure!) One day they wheeled in a machine the size of a table saw. It was an educational computer made for high schools, called the ECP-18. Our school was getting a two-week demo.

I stood in the background as the teachers and technicians talked. This machine had a 15-bit word (*what's a word?*) and a 1024-word drum memory. (I knew what drum memory was by then, but only in concept.)

When they powered it up, it made a whining sound reminiscent of a jet aircraft taking off. I guessed that was the drum spinning up. Once up to speed, it was relatively quiet.

The machine was *lovely*. It was essentially an office desk with a marvelous control panel protruding from the top like the bridge of a battleship. The control panel was adorned with rows of lights that were also push-buttons. Sitting at that desk was like sitting in Captain Kirk's chair.

As I watched the technicians push those buttons, I noted that they lit up when pushed, and that you could push them again to turn them off. I also noted that there were other buttons they were pushing; buttons with names like *deposit* and *run*.

The buttons in each row were grouped into five clusters of three. My Digi-Comp was also three bits, so I could read an octal digit when expressed in binary. It was not a big leap to realize that these were just five octal digits.

As the technicians pushed the buttons I could hear them mutter to themselves. They would push 1, 5, 2, 0, 4, in the *memory buffer* row while saying to themselves, "store in 204." They would push 1, 0, 2, 1, 3 and mutter, "load 213 into the *accumulator*." There was a row of buttons named *accumulator!*

Ten minutes of that and it was pretty clear to my fifteen-year-old mind that the 15 meant *store* and the 10 meant *load*, that the accumulator was what was being stored or loaded, and that the other numbers were the numbers of one of the 1024 words on the drum. (So *that's* what a word is!)

Bit by bit (no pun intended) my eager mind latched on to more and more instruction codes and concepts. By the time the technicians left, I knew the basics of how that machine worked.

That afternoon, during a study hall, I crept into the math lab and started fiddling with the computer. I had learned long ago that it is better to ask forgiveness than permission! I toggled in a little program that would multiply the accumulator by two and add one. I toggled a 5 into the accumulator, ran the program, and saw 13_8 in the accumulator! It had worked!

I toggled in several other simple programs like that and they all worked as planned. I was master of the universe!

Days later I realized how stupid, and lucky, I had been. I found an instruction sheet laying around in the math lab. It showed all the different instructions and op-codes, including many I had not learned by watching the technicians. I was gratified that I had interpreted those that I knew correctly and thrilled by the others. However, one of the new instructions was HLT. It just so happened that the *halt* instruction was a word of all zeros. And it just so happened that I had put a word of all zeros at the end of each of my programs so that I could load it into the accumulator to clear it. The concept of a halt simply had not occurred to me. I just figured the program would stop when it was done!

I remember at one point sitting in the math lab watching one of the teachers struggle to get a program working. He was trying to type two numbers in decimal on the attached teletype, and then print out the sum. Anyone who has tried to write a program like this in machine language on a mini-computer knows that it is far from trivial. You have to read in the characters, convert them to digits, then to binary, add them, convert back to decimal and encode back into characters. And, believe me, it's a *lot* worse when you are entering the program in binary through the front panel!

I watched as he put a halt into his program and then ran it until it stopped. (Oh! That's a good idea!) This primitive breakpoint allowed him to examine the contents of the registers to see what his program had done. I remember him muttering, "Wow, that was fast!" Boy, do I have news for him!

I had no idea what his algorithm was. That kind of programming was still magic to me. And he never spoke to me while I watched over his shoulder. Indeed, *nobody* talked to me about this computer. I think they considered me a nuisance to be ignored, fluttering around the math lab like a moth. Suffice it to say that neither the student nor the teachers had developed a high degree of social skill.

In the end he got his program working. It was amazing to watch. He'd slowly type in the two numbers because, despite his earlier protestation, that computer was *not* fast (think of reading consecutive words from a spinning drum in 1967). When he hit return after the second number, the computer blinked ferociously for a bit and then started to print the result. It took about one second per digit. It printed all but the last digit, blinked even more ferociously for five seconds, and then printed the final digit and halted.

Why that pause before the last digit? I never found out. But it made me realize that the approach to a problem can have a profound effect on the user. Even though the program produced the correct answer, there was *still* something wrong with it.

This was mentoring. Certainly it was not the kind of mentoring I could have hoped for. It would have been nice if one of those teachers had taken me under his wing and worked with me. But it didn't matter, because I was *observing* them and learning at a furious pace.

UNCONVENTIONAL MENTORING

I told you those two stories because they describe two very different kinds of mentoring, neither of which are the kind that the word usually implies. In the first case I learned from the authors of a very well-written manual. In the second case I learned by observing people who were actively trying to ignore me. In both cases the knowledge gained was profound and foundational.

Of course, I had other kinds of mentors too. There was the kindly neighbor who worked at Teletype who brought me home a box of 30 telephone relays to play with. Let me tell you, give a lad some relays and a electric train transformer and he can conquer the world!

There was the kindly neighbor who was a ham operator who showed me how to use a multimeter (which I promptly broke). There was the office supply store owner who allowed me to come in and "play" with his very expensive programmable calculator. There was the Digital Equipment Corporation sales office that allowed me to come in and "play" with their PDP-8 and PDP-10.

Then there was big Jim Carlin, a BAL programmer who saved me from being fired from my first programming job by helping me debug a Cobol program that was way beyond my depth. He taught me how to read core dumps, and how to format my code with appropriate blank lines, rows of stars, and comments. He gave me my first push towards craftsmanship. I'm sorry I could not return the favor when the boss's displeasure fell on him a year later.

But, frankly, that's about it. There just weren't that many senior programmers in the early seventies. Everywhere else I worked, I *was* senior. There was nobody to help me figure out what true professional programming was. There was no role model who taught me how to behave or what to value. Those things I had to learn for myself, and it was by no means easy.

HARD KNOCKS

As I told you before, I did, in fact, get fired from that factory automation job in 1976. Although I was technically very competent, I had not learned to pay attention to the business or the business goals. Dates and deadlines meant nothing to me. I forgot about a big Monday morning demo, left the system broken on Friday, and showed up late on Monday with everyone staring angrily at me.

My boss sent me a letter warning me that I had to make changes immediately or be fired. This was a significant wake-up call for me. I reevaluated my life and career and started to make some significant changes in my behavior—some of which you have been reading about in this book. But it was too little, too late. The momentum was all in the wrong direction and small things that wouldn't have mattered before became significant. So, though I gave it a hardy try, they eventually escorted me out of the building.

Needless to say, it's not fun to bring that kind of news home to a pregnant wife and a two-year old daughter. But I picked myself up and took some powerful life lessons to my next job—which I held for fifteen years and which formed the true foundation of my current career.

In the end, I survived and prospered. But there has to be a better way. It would have been far better for me if I'd had a true mentor, someone to teach me the in's and out's. Someone I could have observed while I helped him with small tasks, and who would review and guide my early work. Someone to act as a role model and teach me appropriate values and reflexes. A sensei. A master. A mentor.

APPRENTICESHIP

What do doctors do? Do you think hospitals hire medical graduates and throw them into operating rooms to do heart surgery on their first day on the job? Of course not.

The medical profession has developed a discipline of intense mentoring ensconced in ritual and lubricated with tradition. The medical profession oversees the universities and makes sure the graduates have the best education. That education involves roughly *equal amounts* of classroom study and clinical activity in hospitals working with professionals.

Upon graduation, and before they can be licensed, the newly minted doctors are required to spend a year in supervised practice and training called internship.

This is intense on-the-job training. The intern is surrounded by role models and teachers.

Once internship has been completed each of the medical specialties requires three to five more years of further supervised practice and training known as residency. The resident gains confidence by taking on ever greater responsibilities while still being surrounded by, and supervised by, senior doctors.

Many specialties require yet another one to three years of fellowship in which the student continues specialized training and supervised practice.

And *then* they are eligible to take their exams and become board certified.

This description of the medical profession was somewhat idealized, and probably wildly inaccurate. But the fact remains that when the stakes are high, we do not send graduates into a room, throw meat in occasionally, and expect good things to come out. So why do we do this in software?

It's true that there are relatively few deaths caused by software bugs. But there *are* significant monetary losses. Companies lose huge amounts of money due to the inadequate training of their software developers.

Somehow the software development industry has gotten the idea that programmers are programmers, and that once you graduate you can code. Indeed, it is not at all uncommon for companies to hire kids right out of school, form them into "teams," and ask them to build the most critical systems. It's insane!

Painters don't do this. Plumbers don't. Electricians don't. Hell, I don't even think short-order cooks behave this way! It seems to me that companies who hire CS graduates ought to invest more in their training than McDonalds invests in their servers.

Let's not kid ourselves that this doesn't matter. There's a lot at stake. Our civilization runs on software. It is software that moves and manipulates the information that pervades our daily life. Software controls our automobile engines, transmissions, and brakes. It maintains our bank balances, sends us our bills, and accepts our payments. Software washes our clothes and tells us the time. It puts pictures on the TV, sends our text messages, makes our phone calls, and entertains us when we are bored. It's everywhere.

Given that we entrust software developers with all aspects of our lives, from the minutia to the momentous, I suggest that a reasonable period of training and supervised practice is not inappropriate.

SOFTWARE APPRENTICESHIP

So how *should* the software profession induct young graduates into the ranks of professionalism? What steps should they follow? What challenges should they meet? What goals should they achieve? Let's work it backwards.

Masters

These are programmers who have taken the lead on more than one significant software project. Typically they will have 10+ years of experience and will have worked on several different kinds of systems, languages, and operating systems. They know how to lead and coordinate multiple teams, are proficient designers and architects, and can code circles around everyone else without breaking a sweat. They have been offered management positions, but have either turned them down, have fled back after accepting them, or have integrated them with their primarily technical role. They maintain that technical role by reading, studying, practicing, doing, and *teaching*. It is to a master that the company will assign technical responsibility for a project. Think, "Scotty."

Journeymen

These are programmers who are trained, competent, and energetic. During this period of their career they will learn to work well in a team and to become team leaders. They are knowledgeable about current technology but typically lack experience with many diverse systems. They tend to know one language, one system, one platform; but they are learning more. Experience levels vary widely among their ranks, but the average is about five years. On the far side of that average we have burgeoning masters; on the near side we have recent apprentices.

Journeymen are supervised by masters, or other more senior journeymen. Young journeymen are seldom allowed autonomy. Their work is closely supervised. Their code is scrutinized. As they gain in experience, autonomy grows. Supervision becomes less direct and more nuanced. Eventually it transitions into peer review.

Apprentices/Interns

Graduates start their careers as apprentices. Apprentices have no autonomy. They are very closely supervised by journeymen. At first they take no tasks at all, they simply provide assistance to the journeymen. This should be a time of very intense pair-programming. This is when disciplines are learned and reinforced. This is when the foundation of values is created.

Journeymen are the teachers. They make sure that the apprentices know design principles, design patterns, disciplines, and rituals. Journeymen teach TDD, refactoring, estimation, and so forth. They assign reading, exercises, and practices to the apprentices; they review their progress.

Apprenticeship ought to last a year. By that time, if the journeymen are willing to accept the apprentice into their ranks, they will make a recommendation to the masters. The masters should examine the apprentice both by interview and by reviewing their accomplishments. If the masters agree, then the apprentice becomes a journeyman.

THE REALITY

Again, all of this is idealized and hypothetical. However, if you change the names and squint at the words you'll realize that it's not all that different from the way we *expect* things to work now. Graduates are supervised by young team-leads, who are supervised by project-leads, and so on. The problem is that, in most cases, this supervision *is not technical!* In most companies there is no technical supervision at all. Programmers get raises and eventual promotions because, well, that's just what you do with programmers.

The difference between what we do today and my idealized program of apprenticeship is the focus on technical teaching, training, supervision, and review.

The difference is the very notion that professional values and technical acumen must be taught, nurtured, nourished, coddled, and encultured. What's missing from our current sterile approach is the responsibility of the elders to teach the young.

CRAFTSMANSHIP

So now we are in a position to define this word: *craftsmanship*. Just what is it? To understand, let's look at the word *craftsman*. This word brings to mind skill and quality. It evokes experience and competence. A craftsman is someone who works quickly, but without rushing, who provides reasonable estimates and meets commitments. A craftsman knows when to say no, but tries hard to say yes. A craftsman is a professional.

Craftsmanship is the *mindset* held by craftsmen. Craftsmanship is a meme that contains values, disciplines, techniques, attitudes, and answers.

But how do cratftsmen adopt this meme? How do they attain this mindset?

The craftsmanship meme is handed from one person to another. It is taught by elders to the young. It is exchanged between peers. It is observed and relearned, as elders observe the young. Craftsmanship is a contagion, a kind of mental virus. You catch it by observing others and allowing the meme to take hold.

CONVINCING PEOPLE

You can't convince people to be craftsmen. You can't convince them to accept the craftsmanship meme. Arguments are ineffective. Data is inconsequential. Case studies mean nothing. The acceptance of a meme is not so much a rational decision as an emotional one. This is a very *human* thing.

So how do you get people to adopt the craftsmanship meme? Remember that a meme is contagious, but only if it can be observed. So you make the meme *observable*. You act as a role model. You become a craftsman first, and let your craftsmanship show. Then just let the meme do the rest of the work.

CONCLUSION

School can teach the theory of computer programming. But school does not, and cannot teach the discipline, practice, and skill of being a craftsman. Those things are acquired through years of personal tutelage and mentoring. It is time for those of us in the software industry to face the fact that guiding the next batch of software developers to maturity will fall to us, not to the universities. It's time for us to adopt a program of apprenticeship, internship, and long-term guidance.

 Tooling

In 1978, I was working at Teradyne on the telephone test system that I described earlier. The system was about 80KSLOC of M365 assembler. We kept the source code on tapes.

The tapes were similar to those 8-track stereo tape cartridges that were so popular back in the '70s. The tape was an endless loop, and the tape drive could only move in one direction. The cartridges came in 10', 25', 50', and 100' lengths. The longer the tape, the longer it took to "rewind" since the tape drive had to simply move it forward until it found the "load point." A 100' tape took five minutes to go to load point, so we chose the lengths of our tapes judiciously.[1]

---

1. These tapes could only be moved in one direction. So when there was a read error, there was no way for the tape drive to back up and read again. You had to stop what you were doing, send the tape back to the load point, and then start again. This happened two or three times per day. Write errors were also very common, and the drive had no way to detect them. So we always wrote the tapes in pairs and then checked the pairs when we were done. If one of the tapes was bad we immediately made a copy. If both were bad, which was very infrequent, we started the whole operation over. That was what life was like in the '70s.

Logically, the tapes were subdivided into files. You could have as many files on a tape as would fit. To find a file you loaded the tape and then skipped forward one file at a time until you found the one you wanted. We kept a listing of the source code directory on the wall so that we would know how many files to skip before we got to the one we wanted.

There was a master 100' copy of the source code tape on a shelf in the lab. It was labeled MASTER. When we wanted to edit a file we loaded the MASTER source tape into one drive and a 10' blank into another. We'd skip through the MASTER until we got to the file we needed. Then we'd copy that file onto the scratch tape. Then we'd "rewind" both tapes and put the MASTER back on the shelf.

There was a special directory listing of the MASTER on a bulletin board in the lab. Once we had made the copies of the files we needed to edit, we'd put a colored pin on the board next to the name of that file. That's how we checked files out!

We edited the tapes on a screen. Our text editor, ED-402, was actually very good. It was very similar to vi. We would read a "page" from tape, edit the contents, and then write that page out and read the next one. A page was typically 50 lines of code. You could not look ahead on the tape to see the pages that were coming, and you could not look back on the tape to see the pages you had edited. So we used listings.

Indeed, we would mark up our listings with all the changes we wanted to make, and *then* we'd edit the files according to our markups. *Nobody* wrote or modified code at the terminal! That was suicide.

Once the changes were made to all the files we needed to edit, we'd merge those files with the master to create a working tape. This is the tape we'd use to run our compiles and tests.

Once we were done testing and were sure our changes worked, we'd look at the board. If there were no new pins on the board we'd simply relabel our working tape as MASTER and pull our pins off the board. If there *were* new pins on the board we'd remove our pins and hand our working tape to the person whose pins were still on the board. They'd have to do the merge.

There were three of us, and each of us had our own color of pin, so it was easy for us to know who had which files checked out. And since we all worked in the same lab and talked to each other all the time, we held the status of the board in our heads. So usually the board was redundant, and we often didn't use it.

TOOLS

Today software developers have a wide array of tools to choose from. Most aren't worth getting involved with, but there are a few that every software developer must be conversant with. This chapter describes my current personal toolkit. I have not done a complete survey of all the other tools out there, so this should not be considered a comprehensive review. This is just what I use.

SOURCE CODE CONTROL

When it comes to source code control, the open source tools are usually your best option. Why? Because they are written by developers, for developers. The open source tools are what developers write for themselves when they need something that works.

There are quite a few expensive, commercial, "enterprise" version control systems available. I find that these are not sold to developers so much as they are sold to managers, executives, and "tool groups." Their list of features is impressive and compelling. Unfortunately, they often don't have the features that developers actually need. The chief among those is *speed*.

AN "ENTERPRISE" SOURCE CONTROL SYSTEM

It may be that your company has invested a small fortune in an "enterprise" source code control system. If so, my condolences. It's probably politically inappropriate for you to go around telling everyone, "Uncle Bob says not to use it." However, there is an easy solution.

You can check your source code into the "enterprise" system at the end of each iteration (once every two weeks or so) and use one of the open source systems in the midst of each iteration. This keeps everyone happy, doesn't violate any corporate rules, and keeps your productivity high.

PESSIMISTIC VERSUS OPTIMISTIC LOCKING

Pessimistic locking seemed like a good idea in the '80s. After all, the simplest way to manage concurrent update problems is to serialize them. So if *I'm* editing a file, *you'd* better not. Indeed, the system of colored pins that I used in the late '70s was a form of pessimistic locking. If there was a pin in a file, you didn't edit that file.

Of course, pessimistic locking has its problems. If I lock a file and then go on vacation, everybody else who wants to edit that file is stuck. Indeed, even if I keep the file locked for a day or two, I can delay others who need to make changes.

Our tools have gotten much better at merging source files that have been edited concurrently. It's actually quite amazing when you think about it. The tools look at the two different files and at the ancestor of those two files, and then they apply multiple strategies to figure out how to integrate the concurrent changes. And they do a pretty good job.

So the era of pessimistic locking is over. We do not need to lock files when we check them out anymore. Indeed, we don't bother to check out individual files at all. We just check out the whole system and edit any files we need to.

When we are ready to check in our changes, we perform an "update" operation. This tells us whether anybody else checked in code ahead of us, automatically merges most of the changes, finds conflicts, and helps us do the remaining merges. Then we commit the merged code.

I'll have a lot to say about the role that automated tests and continuous integration play with regard to this process later on in this chapter. For the moment let's just say that we *never* check in code that doesn't pass all the tests. *Never ever.*

CVS/SVN

The old standby source control system is CVS. It was good for its day but has grown a bit long in the tooth for today's projects. Although it is very good at dealing with individual files and directories, it's not very good at renaming files or deleting directories. And the attic …. . Well, the less said about that, the better.

Subversion, on the other hand, works very nicely. It allows you to check out the whole system in a single operation. You can easily update, merge, and commit. As long as you don't get into branching, SVN systems are pretty simple to manage.

Branching

Until 2008 I avoided all but the simplest forms of branching. If a developer created a branch, that branch had to be brought back into the main line before the end of the iteration. Indeed, I was so austere about branching that it was very rarely done in the projects I was involved with.

If you are using SVN, then I still think that's a good policy. However, there are some new tools that change the game completely. They are the *distributed* source control systems. `git` is my favorite of the distributed source control systems. Let me tell you about it.

git

I started using `git` in late 2008, and it has since changed everything about the way I use source code control. Understanding why this tool is such a game changer is beyond the scope of this book. But comparing Figure A-1 to Figure A-2 ought to be worth quite a few of the words that I'm not going to include here.

Figure A-1 shows a few weeks' worth of development on the FitNesse project while it was controlled by SVN. You can see the effect of my austere no-branching rule. We simply did not branch. Instead, we did very frequent updates, merges, and commits to the main line.

- More bug fixes
- Docs now say that Java 1.5 is required.
- Bug fix
- Many usability and behaviorial improvements.
- Clean up
- Added PAGE_NAME and PAGE_PATH to pre-defined variables.
- Added ** to !path widget.
- link to the fixture gallery
- fixture gallery release 2.0 (2008-06-09) copied into the trunk wiki at
- Firefox compatability for invisible collapsible sections; removed .ce
- Updated documentation suite for all changes since last release.
- Enhancement to handle nulls in saved and recalled symbols. Adde
- Added a "Prune" Properties attribute to exclude a page and its chilc
- Fixed type-o
- Added check for existing child page on rename.
- Added "Rename" link to Symbolic Links property section; renamed
- Adjusted page properties on recently added pages such that they c
- Enhanced Symbolic Links to allow all relative and absolute path for
- Cleaned up renamPageReponder a bit more.
- Cleaned Up PathParser names a bit. Pop -> RemoveNameFromE
- Cleaned up RenamePageResponder a bit. Fixed TestContentsHel|
- updated usage message
- Fixed a bug wherein variables defined in a parent's preformatted bl
- Added explicit responder "getPage" to render a page in case query
- Tweaks to TOC help text.
- New property: Help text; TOCWidget has rollover balloon with new
- Redundant to the JUnit tests and elemental acceptance tests.
- Removed the last of the [acd] tags.
- !contents -f option enhancement to show suite filters in TOC list; fix
- TOC enhancements for properties (-p and PROPERTY_TOC and F
- 1) Render the tags on non-WikiWord links;
- Added http:// prefix to google.com for firewall transparency.
- Isolate query action from additional query arguments. For example
- Accommodate query strings like "?suite&suiteFilter=X"; prior logic v
- Cleaned up AliasLinkWidget a bit.

Figure A-1 FITNESSE under subversion

Figure A-2 picture shows a few weeks' worth of development on the same project using git. As you can see, we are branching and merging all over the place. This was not because I relaxed my no-branching policy; rather, it simply

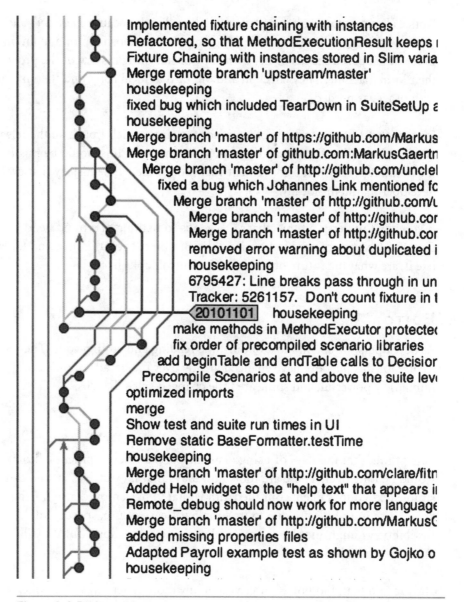

Implemented fixture chaining with instances
Refactored, so that MethodExecutionResult keeps
Fixture Chaining with instances stored in Slim varia
Merge remote branch 'upstream/master'
housekeeping
fixed bug which included TearDown in SuiteSetUp a
housekeeping
Merge branch 'master' of https://github.com/Markus
Merge branch 'master' of github.com:MarkusGaertn
Merge branch 'master' of http://github.com/unclel
fixed a bug which Johannes Link mentioned fc
Merge branch 'master' of http://github.com/u
Merge branch 'master' of http://github.cor
Merge branch 'master' of http://github.cor
removed error warning about duplicated i
housekeeping
6795427: Line breaks pass through in un
Tracker: 5261157. Don't count fixture in i
20101101   housekeeping
make methods in MethodExecutor protectec
fix order of precompiled scenario libraries
add beginTable and endTable calls to Decisior
Precompile Scenarios at and above the suite leve
optimized imports
merge
Show test and suite run times in UI
Remove static BaseFormatter.testTime
housekeeping
Merge branch 'master' of http://github.com/clare/fitr
Added Help widget so the "help text" that appears ir
Remote_debug should now work for more language
Merge branch 'master' of http://github.com/MarkusG
added missing properties files
Adapted Payroll example test as shown by Gojko o
housekeeping

Figure A-2 FITNESSE under git

became the obvious and most convenient way to work. Individual developers can make very short-lived branches and then merge them with each other on a whim.

Notice also that you can't see a true main line. That's because *there isn't one.* When you use git there's no such thing as a central repository, or a main line. Every developer keeps his or her own copy of the *entire* history of the project on their local machine. They check in and out of that local copy, and then merge it with others as needed.

It's true that I keep a special golden repository into which I push all the releases and interim builds. But to call this repository the main line would be missing the point. It's really just a convenient snapshot of the whole history that every developer maintains locally.

If you don't understand this, that's OK. git is something of a mind bender at first. You have to get used to how it works. But I'll tell you this: git, and tools like it, are what the future of source code control looks like.

IDE/Editor

As developers, we spend most of our time reading and editing code. The tools we use for this purpose have changed greatly over the decades. Some are immensely powerful, and some are little changed since the '70s.

VI

You'd think that the days of using vi as the primary development editor would be long over. There are tools nowadays that far outclass vi, and other simple text editors like it. But the truth is that vi has enjoyed a significant resurgence in popularity due to its simplicity, ease of use, speed, and flexibility. Vi might not be as powerful as Emacs, or eclipse, but it's still a fast and powerful editor.

Having said that, I'm not a power vi user any more. There was a day when I was known as a vi "god," but those days are long gone. I use vi from time to time if I need to do a quick edit of a text file. I have even used it recently to make a quick change to a Java source file in a remote environment. But the amount of true coding I have done in vi in the last 10 years is vanishingly small.

Emacs

Emacs is still one of the most powerful editors out there, and will probably remain so for decades to come. The internal lisp model guarantees that. As a general-purpose editing tool, nothing else even comes close. On the other hand, I think that Emacs cannot really compete with the specific-purpose IDEs that now dominate. Editing code is *not* a general-purpose editing job.

In the '90s I was an Emacs bigot. I wouldn't consider using anything else. The point-and-click editors of the day were laughable toys that no developer could take seriously. But in the early '00s I was introduced to IntelliJ, my current IDE of choice, and I've never looked back.

Eclipse/IntelliJ

I'm an IntelliJ user. I love it. I use it to write Java, Ruby, Clojure, Scala, Javascript, and many others. This tool was written by programmers who understand what programmers need when writing code. Over the years, they have seldom disappointed me and almost always pleased me.

Eclipse is similar in power and scope to IntelliJ. The two are simply leaps and bounds above Emacs when it comes to editing Java. There are other IDEs in this category, but I won't mention them here because I have no direct experience with them.

The features that set these IDEs above tools like Emacs are the extremely powerful ways in which they help you manipulate code. In IntelliJ, for example, you can extract a superclass from a class with a single command. You can rename variables, extract methods, and convert inheritance into composition, among many other great features.

With these tools, code editing is no longer about lines and characters as much as it is about complex manipulations. Rather than thinking about the next few characters and lines you need to type, you think about the next few trans-formations you need to make. In short, the programming model is remarkably different and highly productive.

Of course, this power comes at a cost. The learning curve is high, and project set-up time is not insignificant. These tools are *not* lightweight. They take a lot of computing resources to run.

TextMate

TextMate is powerful and lightweight. It can't do the wonderful manipulations that IntelliJ and Eclipse can do. It doesn't have the powerful lisp engine and library of Emacs. It doesn't have the speed and fluidity of vi. On the other hand, the learning curve is small, and its operation is intuitive.

I use TextMate from time to time, especially for the occasional C++. I would use Emacs for a large C++ project, but I'm too rusty to bother with Emacs for the short little C++ tasks I have.

Issue Tracking

At the moment I'm using Pivotal Tracker. It's an elegant and simple system to use. It fits nicely with the Agile/iterative approach. It allows all the stakeholders and developers to communicate quickly. I'm very pleased with it.

For very small projects, I've sometimes used Lighthouse. It's very quick and easy to set up and use. But it doesn't come close to the power of Tracker.

I've also simply used a wiki. Wikis are fine for internal projects. They allow you to set up any scheme you like. You aren't forced into a certain process or a rigid structure. They are very easy to understand and use.

Sometimes the best issue-tracking system of all is a set of cards and a bulletin board. The bulletin board is divided into columns such as "To Do," "In Progress," and "Done." The developers simply move the cards from one column to the next when appropriate. Indeed, this may be the most common issue-tracking system used by agile teams today.

The recommendation I make to clients is to start with a manual system like the bulletin board before you purchase a tracking tool. Once you've mastered the manual system, you will have the knowledge you need to select the appropriate tool. And indeed, the appropriate choice may simply be to continue using the manual system.

BUG COUNTS

Teams of developers certainly need a list of issues to work on. Those issues include new tasks and features as well as bugs. For any reasonably sized team (5 to 12 developers) the size of that list should be in the dozens to hundreds. *Not thousands.*

If you have thousands of bugs, something is wrong. If you have thousands of features and/or tasks, something is wrong. In general, the list of issues should be relatively small, and therefore manageable with a lightweight tool like a wiki, Lighthouse, or Tracker.

There are some commercial tools out there that seem to be pretty good. I've seen clients use them but haven't had the opportunity to work with them directly. I am not opposed to tools like this, as long as the number of issues remains small and manageable. When issue-tracking tools are forced to track thousands of issues, then the word "tracking" loses meaning. They become "issue dumps" (and often smell like a dump too).

CONTINUOUS BUILD

Lately I've been using Jenkins as my Continuous Build engine. It's lightweight, simple, and has almost no learning curve. You download it, run it, do some quick and simple configurations, and you are up and running. Very nice.

My philosophy about continuous build is simple: Hook it up to your source code control system. Whenever anybody checks in code, it should automatically build and then report status to the team.

The team must simply keep the build working at all times. If the build fails, it should be a "stop the presses" event and the team should meet to quickly resolve the issue. Under no circumstances should the failure be allowed to persist for a day or more.

For the FITNESSE project I have every developer run the continuous-build script before they commit. The build takes less than 5 minutes, so this is not onerous. If there are problems, the developers resolve them before the commit. So the automatic build seldom has any problems. The most common source of automatic build failures turns out to be environment-related issues since my automatic build environment is quite different from the developer's development environments.

UNIT TESTING TOOLS

Each language has it's own particular unit testing tool. My favorites are JUnit for Java, RSPEC for Ruby, NUnit for .Net, Midje for Clojure, and CPPUTEST for C and C++.

Whatever unit testing tool you choose, there are a few basic features they all should support.

1. It should be quick and easy to run the tests. Whether this is done through IDE plugins or simple command line tools is irrelevant, as long as developers can run those tests on a whim. The gesture to run the tests should be trivial.

    For example, I run my CPPUTEST tests by typing command-M in TextMate. I have this command set up to run my makefile which automatically runs the tests and prints a one-line report if all tests pass. JUnit and RSPEC are both supported by INTELLIJ, so all I have to do is push a button. For NUnit, I use the RESHARPER plugin to give me the test button.

2. The tool should give you a clear visual pass/fail indication. It doesn't matter if this is a graphical green bar or a console message that says "All Tests Pass." The point is that you must be able to tell that all tests passed quickly and unambiguously. If you have to read a multiline report, or worse, compare the output of two files to tell whether the tests passed, then you have failed this point.

3. The tool should give you a clear visual indication of progress. It doesn't matter whether this is a graphical meter or a string of dots as long as you can tell that progress is still being made and that the tests have not stalled or aborted.

4. The tool should discourage individual test cases from communicating with each other. JUNIT does this by creating a new instance of the test class for each test method, thereby preventing the tests from using instance variables to communicate with each other. Other tools will run the test methods in random order so that you can't depend on one test preceding another. Whatever the mechanism, the tool should help you keep your tests independent from each other. Dependent tests are a deep trap that you don't want to fall into.

5. The tool should make it very easy to write tests. JUNIT does this by supplying a convenient API for making assertions. It also uses reflection and Java attributes to distinguish test functions from normal functions. This allows a good IDE to automatically identify all your tests, eliminating the hassle of wiring up suites and creating error-prone lists of tests.

COMPONENT TESTING TOOLS

These tools are for testing components at the API level. Their role is to make sure that the behavior of a component is specified in a language that the business and QA people can understand. Indeed, the ideal case is when business analysts and QA can *write* that specification using the tool.

THE DEFINITION OF *DONE*

More than any other tool, component testing tools are the means by which we specify what *done* means. When business analysts and QA collaborate to create a specification that defines the behavior of a component, and when that specification can be executed as a suite of tests that pass or fail, then *done* takes on a very unambiguous meaning: "All Tests Pass."

FITNESSE

My favorite component testing tool is FITNESSE. I wrote a large part of it, and I am the primary committer. So it's my baby.

FITNESSE is a wiki-based system that allows business analysts and QA specialists to write tests in a very simple tabular format. These tables are similar to Parnas tables both in form and intent. The tests can be quickly assembled into suites, and the suites can be run at a whim.

FITNESSE is written in Java but can test systems in any language because it communicates with an underlying test system that can be written in any language. Supported languages include Java, C#/.NET, C, C++, Python, Ruby, PHP, Delphi, and others.

There are two test systems that underlie FITNESSE: Fit and Slim. Fit was written by Ward Cunningham and was the original inspiration for FITNESSE and it's ilk. Slim is a much simpler and more portable test system that is favored by FITNESSE users today.

OTHER TOOLS

I know of several other tools that could classify as component testing tools.

- RobotFX is a tool developed by Nokia engineers. It uses a similar tabular format to FITNESSE, but is not wiki based. The tool simply runs on flat files prepared with Excel or similar. The tool is written in Python but can test systems in any language using appropriate bridges.
- Green Pepper is a commercial tool that has a number of similarities with FITNESSE. It is based on the popular confluence wiki.
- Cucumber is a plain text tool driven by a Ruby engine, but capable of testing many different platforms. The language of Cucumber is the popular Given/When/Then style.
- JBehave is similar to Cucumber and is the logical parent of Cucumber. It is written in Java.

INTEGRATION TESTING TOOLS

Component testing tools can also be used for many integration tests, but are less than appropriate for tests that are driven through the UI.

In general, we don't want to drive very many tests through the UI because UIs are notoriously volatile. That volatility makes tests that go through the UI very fragile.

Having said that, there are some tests that *must* go through the UI—most importantly, tests *of* the UI. Also, a few end-to-end tests should go through the whole assembled system, including the UI.

The tools that I like best for UI testing are Selenium and Watir.

UML/MDA

In the early '90s I was very hopeful that the CASE tool industry would cause a radical change in the way software developers worked. As I looked ahead from those heady days, I thought that by now everyone would be coding in diagrams at a higher level of abstraction and that textual code would be a thing of the past.

Boy was I wrong. Not only hasn't this dream been fulfilled, but every attempt to move in that direction has met with abject failure. Not that there aren't tools and systems out there that demonstrate the potential; it's just that those tools simply don't truly realize the dream, and hardly anybody seems to want to use them.

The dream was that software developers could leave behind the details of textual code and author systems in a higher-level language of diagrams. Indeed, so the dream goes, we might not need programmers at all. Architects could create whole systems from UML diagrams. Engines, vast and cool and unsympathetic to the plight of mere programmers, would transform those diagrams into executable code. Such was the grand dream of Model Driven Architecture (MDA).

Unfortunately, this grand dream has one tiny little flaw. MDA assumes that the problem is code. But code is *not* the problem. It has never been the problem. The problem is *detail.*

THE DETAILS

Programmers are detail managers. That's what we do. We specify the behavior of systems in the minutest detail. We happen to use textual languages for this (code) because textual languages are remarkably convenient (consider English, for example).

What kinds of details do we manage?

Do you know the difference between the two characters \n and \r? The first, \n, is a line feed. The second, \r, is a carriage return. What's a carriage?

In the '60s and early '70s one of the more common output devices for computers was a teletype. The model ASR33[2] was the most common.

This device consisted of a print head that could print ten characters per second. The print head was composed of a little cylinder with the characters embossed upon it. The cylinder would rotate and elevate so that the correct character was facing the paper, and then a little hammer would smack the cylinder against the paper. There was an ink ribbon between the cylinder and the paper, and the ink transferred to the paper in the shape of the character.

The print head rode on a carriage. With every character the carriage would move one space to the right, taking the print head with it. When the carriage got to the end of the 72-character line, you had to explicitly return the carriage by sending the carriage return characters ($\r = 0 \times 0D$), otherwise the print head would continue to print characters in the 72nd column, turning it into a nasty black rectangle.

Of course, that wasn't sufficient. Returning the carriage did not raise the paper to the next line. If you returned the carriage and did not send a line-feed character ($\n = 0 \times 0A$), then the new line would print on top of the old line.

Therefore, for an ASR33 teletype the end-of-line sequence was "\r\n". Actually, you had to be careful about that since the carriage might take more than 100ms to return. If you sent "\n\r" then the next character just might get printed as the carriage returned, thereby creating a smudged character in the middle of the line. To be safe, we often padded the end-of-line sequence with one or two rubout[3] characters ($0 \times FF$).

---

2. http://en.wikipedia.org/wiki/ASR-33_Teletype

3. Rubout characters were very useful for editing paper tapes. By convention, rubout characters were ignored. Their code, $0 \times FF$, meant that every hole on that row of the tape was punched. This meant that any character could be converted to a rubout by overpunching it. Therefore, if you made a mistake while typing your program you could backspace the punch and hit *rubout*, then continue typing.

In the '70s, as teletypes began to fade from use, operating systems like UNIX shortened the end-of-line sequence to simply '\n'. However, other operating systems, like DOS, continued to use the '\r\n' convention.

When was the last time you had to deal with text files that use the "wrong" convention? I face this problem at least once a year. Two identical source files don't compare, and don't generate identical checksums, because they use different line ends. Text editors fail to word-wrap properly, or double space the text because the line ends are "wrong." Programs that don't expect blank lines crash because they interpret '\r\n' as two lines. Some programs recognize '\r\n' but don't recognize '\n\r'. And so on.

That's what I mean by *detail*. Try coding the horrible logic for sorting out line ends in UML!

No Hope, No Change

The hope of the MDA movement was that a great deal of detail could be eliminated by using diagrams instead of code. That hope has so far proven to be forlorn. It turns out that there just isn't that much extra detail embedded in code that can be eliminated by pictures. What's more, pictures contain their own accidental details. Pictures have their own grammar and syntax and rules and constraints. So, in the end, the difference in detail is a wash.

The hope of MDA was that diagrams would prove to be at a higher level of abstraction than code, just as Java is at a higher level than assembler. But again, that hope has so far proven to be misplaced. The difference in the level of abstraction is tiny at best.

And, finally, let's say that one day someone does invent a truly useful diagrammatic language. It won't be architects drawing those diagrams, it will be programmers. The diagrams will simply become the new code, and programmers will be needed to *draw* that code because, in the end, it's all about detail, and it is programmers who manage that detail.

Conclusion

Software tools have gotten wildly more powerful and plentiful since I started programming. My current toolkit is a simple subset of that menagerie. I use git for source code control, Tracker for issue management, Jenkins for Continuous Build, IntelliJ as my IDE, XUnit for testing, and FitNesse for component testing.

My machine is a Macbook Pro, 2.8Ghz Intel Core i7, with a 17-inch matte screen, 8GB ram, 512GB SSD, with two extra screens.

INDEX

informIT.com THE TRUSTED TECHNOLOGY LEARNING SOURCE

PEARSON

InformIT is a brand of Pearson and the online presence for the world's leading technology publishers. It's your source for reliable and qualified content and knowledge, providing access to the top brands, authors, and contributors from the tech community.

Addison-Wesley Cisco Press EXAM/CRAM IBM Press. QUe PRENTICE HALL SAMS | Safari

LearnIT at InformIT

Looking for a book, eBook, or training video on a new technology? Seeking timely and relevant information and tutorials? Looking for expert opinions, advice, and tips? **InformIT has the solution.**

- Learn about new releases and special promotions by subscribing to a wide variety of newsletters. Visit **informit.com/newsletters**.

- Access FREE podcasts from experts at **informit.com/podcasts**.

- Read the latest author articles and sample chapters at **informit.com/articles**.

- Access thousands of books and videos in the Safari Books Online digital library at **safari.informit.com**.

- Get tips from expert blogs at **informit.com/blogs**.

Visit **informit.com/learn** to discover all the ways you can access the hottest technology content.

Are You Part of the IT Crowd?

Connect with Pearson authors and editors via RSS feeds, Facebook, Twitter, YouTube, and more! Visit **informit.com/socialconnect**.

informIT.com THE TRUSTED TECHNOLOGY LEARNING SOURCE **PEARSON**

Addison-Wesley Cisco Press EXAM/CRAM IBM Press. QUe PRENTICE HALL SAMS | Safari